FORENSIC SCIENCE

Modern Methods of Solving Crime

Max M. Houck

PRAEGER

Westport, Connecticut
London

Library of Congress Cataloging-in-Publication Data

Houck, Max M.
    Forensic science : modern methods of solving crime / Max M. Houck.
        p. cm.
    Includes bibliographical references and index.
    ISBN 978–0–275–99323–8 (alk. paper)
    1. Forensic sciences. 2. Criminal investigation. I. Title.
    HV8073.H76   2007
    363.25—dc22   2007000060

British Library Cataloguing in Publication Data is available.

Library of Congress Catalog Card Number: 2007000060
ISBN-10: 0–275–99323–X
ISBN-13: 978–0–275–99323–8

First published in 2007

Praeger Publishers, 88 Post Road West, Westport, CT 06881
An imprint of Greenwood Publishing Group, Inc.
www.praeger.com

Printed in the United States of America

The paper used in this book complies with the
Permanent Paper Standard issued by the National
Information Standards Organization (Z39.48–1984).

10   9   8   7   6   5   4   3   2   1

This book is dedicated to all of the students in my courses at West Virginia University who deserve sincere thanks for helping me understand, reduce, and refine the fundamentals of what forensic science is. Students are always the best teachers—that's my story and I'll stick by it.

Contents

Preface

In the "Introduction to Forensic Science" course I teach at West Virginia University, I try to jog the students' minds from their preconceptions, especially about the forensic sciences. I explain how forensic science is a historical science, like geology, archaeology, or astronomy, and forensic scientists reconstruct past criminal events through physical evidence. This reconstruction requires an interpretation or telling of the events (a "strong narrative") and this, in turn, requires a grammar. If nouns are the sources of the evidence (guns, sweaters, bodies, etc.), the bits of evidence found at the scene or on the victim are pronouns (representing as they do the subjects or objects, i.e., nouns or evidence), and the criminals' actions themselves are the verbs. Adjectives and adverbs come infrequently to forensic interpretations unless they are bound within the factual description of the evidence—portions of snapshots, frozen partial views of the past criminal events. A perfect reconstruction of a crime scene would be an infinitely detailed video, capable of being enhanced, reviewed, and reanalyzed at the whim of the investigating scientist. Forensic science does not get evidence like this, not even *video* evidence. The "partial snapshot" analogy encourages them to consider what can and cannot be said after a forensic analysis—it encourages conservatism. It also frames the students actions themselves are the verbs. Adjectives and adverbs come infrequently to forensic interpretations unless they are bound within the factual description of the evidence—portions of snapshots, frozen partial views of the past criminal events. A perfect reconstruction of a crime scene would be an infinitely detailed video, capable of being enhanced, reviewed, and reanalyzed at the whim of the investigating scientist. Forensic science does not get evidence like this, not even *video* evidence. The "partial snapshot" analogy encourages them to consider what can and cannot be said after a forensic analysis—it encourages conservatism. It also frames the students view of forensic science outside the traditional perspective and they realize they can play with ideas a bit more than they might have otherwise considered.

They understand there are things you can and cannot say in forensic science and perhaps also understand why the rules of grammar need to be bent at times. Forensic science is now something other than the media-colored perception with which they started class (M.M. Houck, "CSI: Reality," *Scientific American* [2000]: 84–89).

A drug chemist once argued with me that what my students did was not a "historical science," as I teach my students, because they performed chemical analyses on the suspected illicit drug samples and were not involved in a reconstruction. The substance either was cocaine or not and that was the end of their concern in the matter. Fair enough, as far as that argument goes. But to what end is the chemical analysis being performed? Surely not for the pure joy of chemistry alone. The analysis is done to support or refute the allegation that a person was found with an illegal substance in their possession. Read that sentence again. You probably slipped past the two most important words in that last sentence: *was found*. Possession of cocaine ostensibly indicates a *past criminal act* and the chemist, whether he or she acknowledges it or not, is assisting in the reconstruction of that event.

A bit of explanation about this grammar thing may be necessary. When two things come into contact, information is exchanged. This is one of the central guiding principles of forensic science. Developed by Edmund Locard, it posits that this exchange of information occurs, even if the results are not identifiable or are too small to be found. The results of such a transfer would not be the transfer itself, but the remnants of that transaction, what paleoclimatologists call proxy data. Proxy data that are collected and analyzed by forensic scientists are evidence; if these are not collected or analyzed, they can hardly help to make a proposition more or less likely. Otherwise, these are just proxy data left at the scene of the crime. This is why I call evidence "pronouns": we rarely examine the thing itself *for* itself but examine either bits of it that have transferred or something transferred to it that *represents* the source. Pronouns stand in for nouns and through the context of a sentence we know which "it" or "he" stands for the "toaster" or "John."

Because forensic science demonstrates associations between people, places, and things, essentially *all evidence is transfer evidence.* The following table lists some examples in support of this concept. All evidence comes from a source and ends up on a target; in this sense, all evidence is transferred.

Item	Transferred From (Source)	Transferred To (Target/Location)
Drugs	Dealer	Buyer's pocket or car
Bloodstains	Victim's body	Bedroom wall
Alcohol	Glass	Drunk driver's bloodstream
Semen	Assailant	Victim
Ink	Writer's pen	Stolen check
Handwriting	Writer's hand/brain	Falsified document
Fibers	Kidnapper's car	Victim's jacket
Paint chips/smear	Vehicle	Hit-and-run victim
Bullet	Shooter's gun	Victim's body
Striations	Barrel of shooter's gun	Discharged bullet
Imperfections	Barrel-cutting tool	Shooter's gun's barrel

Not all forensic scientists would agree with this view; nontrace evidence analysts would be among the first to disagree. But it makes sense to my students, who are something of a tabula rasa when they come in (television notwithstanding). In working toward a unified theoretical basis of forensic science, we must be willing to collapse categories as well as to expand them.

Another idea that may not be self-evidenct: Evidence is accidental. Items are transformed into evidence by their involvement in a crime regardless of their source or mode of production. No factories churn out bloody clothing or spent bullets. By becoming evidence, everyday items have their normal meaning enhanced and expanded. Evidence is initially categorized much like the real world; that is, based on the taxonomy created by manufacturers (e.g., optical glass vs. bottle glass) or devised by natural scientists (shale vs. wollastonite, finches vs. pigeons—including subtypes). Forensic science adds to this taxonomy to further enhance or clarify the meaning of evidence relevant to the goals and procedures of the discipline.

Forensic science's taxonomies, while based on production taxonomies, are nevertheless different from them. Manufacturing of economic goods, for example, creates its taxonomy through analytical methods. Standard methods ensure a quality product fit for purpose and sale. The taxonomy is based on the markets involved, the orientation of the company production methods, and the supply web of raw and processed materials.

Explicit rules exist on categories recognized by manufacturers and consumers: McDonald's versus Burger King, loafers versus oxfords, Windows versus Macintosh.

Forensic analytical methods create different taxonomies, however, because forensic scientists have different goals and this requires the use of different methods. Their taxonomies are based on manufactured or class traits, but also aftermarket qualities, intended end use but also "as used." The "as used" traits are those imparted to the item after purchase either through normal use or criminal use. Forensic science has developed a set of rules through which the taxonomies are explicated. For example, forensic scientists are interested in the size, shape, and distribution of delustrants—microscopic grains of titanium dioxide—incorporated into a fiber to reduce its brightness. The product determines the goal; ball gowns should be shiny, carpets should not be. The manufacturer has included delustrants in the fiber at a certain rate and percentage with no concern for shape or distribution (but size may be relevant). The forensic science taxonomy is based on the manufacturing taxonomy but is extended by incidental characteristics that help us to distinguish otherwise similar objects. A heavily delustered fiber may have large or small granules; they may be evenly distributed or clumped together; they may be round or irregular, and so on. The fiber manufacturer could not care less but the forensic scientist cares a great deal.

P.W. Bridgman once wrote, "The concept is synonymous with the corresponding set of observations" (*The Logic of Modern Physics*, 1932, New York: Macmillan Publishers, 5).

Although terse, this phrase is apt for forensic science. Each measurement taken and each observation made are indications of the conceptual principles that support a science. So it is with forensic science—refractive index is useful to an analysis precisely for the reasons it is used: It helps to discriminate between materials. Of course, my bias is evident: I see trace evidence as embodying the essence of forensic science. Perhaps it is not bias, however, but merely the proper viewpoint. After all, "only Nixon could go to China," and maybe what is required to point out the bare philosophical underpinnings of our discipline are the people closest to it's guiding principle. Trace evidence gets short shrift in many of today's forensic laboratories, especially struggling in the shadow of its younger, more popular sibling, DNA.

I hope this book brings a fresh view of forensic science to you, one that is not tinged by accusations of inept practitioners, wildly dramatic television shows, or the rhetoric of attorneys. It is a fascinating field and one that is still in many ways maturing from its adolescence in police agencies. The view I offer will, I hope, spur you to support forensic science in its growth and development as an integral part of the criminal justice system.

MMH

Acknowledgments

Thanking people is a nicety we ignore too often. Writing takes time, solitude, and doggedness; this, in turn, requires the indulgence of people who invest in and count on your presence. Thanks are due to those individuals whose time I have stolen or who have invested in me so that I may steal that time: My wife, Lucy; my father, Max; my staff at the Forensic Science Initiative (Mary, Robin, Samantha, Anna, Emily, Ryan, Marlene, and Shiela); my agent Jodie; and Suzanne Staszak-Silva (we tried). Finally, thanks to you for reading this book.

Important Moments in the History of the Forensic Sciences

1810   Eugène François Vidocq, a noted wily criminal, convinces the Paris police to exchange a jail sentence to become an informant in Paris' toughest prison. Vidocq would eventually establish the first detective force, the Sûreté of Paris.

1828   William Nichol invents the polarizing light microscope, revolutionizing the study of microscopic materials.

1835   Adolphe Quetelet, who based his work on the criminology of Caesare Lombroso, postulates that no two human bodies are exactly alike.

1835   Henry Goddard performs the first forensic bullet comparison. Goddard's work implicates a butler who faked a burglary to commit murder based on similar flaws in a questioned bullet and the mold that made it.

1838   William Stewart of Baltimore murders his father and is convicted based on bullet evidence, making it the first case solved by forensic firearms examination in the United States.

1856   Sir William Herschel, a British officer working for the Indian Civil service, uses fingerprints on documents to verify document signatures, a practice recognized in India but not forensically.

1863   The German scientist Christian Schönbein discovers the oxidation of hydrogen peroxide when exposed to hemoglobin. The foaming reaction is the first presumptive test for blood.

1880   Henry Faulds, a Scottish physician working in Tokyo, publishes a paper in the journal *Nature* suggesting that fingerprints could identify an individual involved in a crime. Faulds goes on to use fingerprints to solve a burglary.

1883   Alphonse Bertillon identifies his first recidivist based on his system of Anthropometry.

1887   Arthur Conan Doyle publishes the first Sherlock Holmes story.

1891   Hans Gross publishes *Handbuch fur Untersuchungsrichter* (Handbook for Examining Magistrates), the first comprehensive text that promotes the use of science and microscopy to solve crimes.

1892   Francis Galton publishes *Fingerprints*, the first text on the nature of fingerprints and their use as a forensic method.

1894   Alfred Dreyfus of France is convicted of treason based on a faulty handwriting identification by Bertillon.

1896   Sir Edward Henry develops a classification system for fingerprints that becomes the standard taxonomy in Europe and North America.

1900   Karl Landsteiner first discovers human blood groups (the ABO system); he is awarded the Nobel prize for this in 1930. Landsteiner's work on blood forms the basis of nearly all subsequent forensic blood work.

1901   Sir Edward Richard Henry is appointed head of Scotland Yard and pushes for the adoption of fingerprints over Bertillon's anthropometry.

1901   Henry DeForrest pioneers the first systematic use of fingerprints in the United States in the New York Civil Service Commission.

1902   Professor R.A. Reiss, professor at the University of Lausanne, Switzerland and a student of Bertillon, pioneers academic curricula in forensic science.

1903   The New York State Prison system begins the systematic use of fingerprints for United States criminal identification.

1908   U.S. President Theodore Roosevelt establishes a Federal Bureau of Investigation (FBI).

1910   Victor Balthazard, professor of forensic medicine at the Sorbonne, with Marcelle Lambert, publishes the first comprehensive hair study, *Le poil de l'homme et des animaux*. In one of the first cases involving hairs, Rosella Rousseau was convinced to confess to murder of Germaine Bichon.

1910   Edmund Locard, successor to Lacassagne as professor of forensic medicine at the University of Lyons, France, establishes the first police crime laboratory.

1913   Victor Balthazard, professor of forensic medicine at the Sorbonne, publishes the first article on individualizing bullet markings.

1915   International Association for Criminal Identification (later to become The International Association of Identification [IAI]) is organized in Oakland, California.

1920   Calvin Goddard, with Charles Waite, Phillip O. Gravelle, and John H. Fisher, perfects the comparison microscope for use in bullet comparison.

1923   In *Frye v. United States*, polygraph test results were ruled inadmissible. The federal ruling introduces the concept of general acceptance and states that polygraph testing does not meet that criterion.

1924   August Vollmer, as chief of police in Los Angeles, California, implements the first U.S. police crime laboratory. U.S. Attorney General Harlan Fiske Stone appoints a young lawyer, J. Edgar Hoover, to "clean house" at the corrupt FBI.

1926   The case of Sacco and Vanzetti popularizes the use of the comparison microscope for bullet comparison.

1932   The FBI establishes its own forensic laboratory.

1937   Paul Kirk assumes leadership of the criminology program at the University of California at Berkeley. In 1945, he finalizes a major in technical criminology.

1950   August Vollmer, chief of police of Berkeley, California, establishes the School of Criminology at the University of California at Berkeley. Paul Kirk presides over the major of Criminalistics within the school.

1950   The American Academy of Forensic Science is formed in Chicago, Illinois. The group also begins publication of the *Journal of Forensic Science*.

1953   Kirk publishes *Crime Investigation*.

1971   Brian Culliford publishes *The Examination and Typing of Bloodstains in the Crime Laboratory*, establishing protocols and standard methods for typing of protein and enzyme markers.

1975   The *Federal Rules of Evidence*, originally promulgated by the U.S. Supreme Court, are enacted as a congressional statute.

1977   The Fourier transform infrared spectrophotometer (FTIR) is adapted for use in the forensic laboratory. The FBI introduces the Automated Fingerprint Identification System (AFIS) with the first digitized scans of fingerprints.

1984   Sir Alec Jeffreys develops the first DNA profiling test. He publishes his findings in *Nature* in 1985.

1986   In the first use of DNA to solve a crime, Jeffreys uses DNA profiling to identify Colin Pitchfork as the murderer of two young girls in England.

1983   The polymerase chain reaction (PCR) is first conceived by Kerry Mullis. The first paper on the technique is not published for two years.

1987   DNA profiling is introduced for the first time in a U.S. criminal court.

1987   *New York v. Castro* is the first case challenging the admissibility of DNA.

1991   Walsh Automation Inc. (now Forensic Technology, Inc.) launches the Integrated Ballistics Identification System, or IBIS, for the automated comparison of fired bullets and cartridge cases. This system is subsequently developed for the United States in collaboration with the Bureau of Alcohol, Tobacco, and Firearms (ATF).

1992   The FBI sponsors development of Drugfire, an automated imaging system to compare marks left on fired cartridge cases.

1993   In *Daubert et al. v. Merrell Dow*, a U.S. federal court refines the standard for admission of scientific evidence.

1996   In *Tennessee v. Ware*, mitochondrial DNA typing is first admitted in a U.S. court.

1998   The National DNA Index System (NDIS), enabling interstate sharing of DNA information to solve crimes, is initiated by the FBI.

1999   IBIS and Drugfire are integrated by the FBI and ATF, creating the National Integrated Ballistics Identification Network (NIBIN).

CHAPTER **1**

History

If you were a detective engaged in tracing a murder, would you expect to find that the murderer had left his photograph behind at the place of the crime, with his address attached? Or would you not necessarily have to be satisfied with comparatively slight and obscure traces of the person you were in search of?

—Sigmund Freud

One of the most admirable things about history is, that almost as a rule we get as much information out of what it does not say as we get out of what it does say. And so, one may truly and axiomatically aver this, to-wit: that history consists of two equal parts; one of these halves is statements of fact, the other half is inference, drawn from the facts.... When the practiced eye of the simple peasant sees the half of a frog projecting above the water, he unerringly infers the half of the frog which he does not see. To the expert student in our great science, history is a frog; half of it is submerged, but he knows it is there, and he knows the shape of it.

—Mark Twain, *The Secret History of Eddypus*

The Oxford English Dictionary lists one of the first uses of the phrase "forensic science" to describe "a mixed science." The early days of forensic science could certainly be called mixed, when science served justice by its application to questions before the court. Forensic science has grown as a profession from the early 1880s and into a science in its own right in the early twenty-first century. Given the public's interest in using science to solve crimes, it looks as if forensic science has an active, even hectic, future.

Forensic science describes the science of associating people, places, and things involved in criminal activities; these scientific disciplines assist in investigating and adjudicating criminal and civil cases. The discipline has two parts to it divides neatly, like the term that describes it.

Science is the collection of systematic methodologies used to increasingly understand the physical world. The word "forensic" is derived from the Latin *forum* meaning "public." In ancient Rome, the Senate met in the Forum, a public place where the political and policy issues of the day were discussed and debated; even today, high school or university teams that compete in debates or public speaking are called "forensics." More technically, forensic means "as applied to public or legal concerns." Together, "forensic science" is an appropriate term for the profession which answers scientific questions for the courts.

Forensic Science Laboratories and Professional Organizations

It may seem odd, but the structure of a forensic science laboratory varies with jurisdiction, agency, and history. Forensic laboratories outside the United States vary even more in their structure; in fact, some are even housed in universities. The analyses and services that a forensic science laboratory provides also vary based on the laboratory's budget, personnel, equipment, and the jurisdiction's crime rate.

The majority of forensic science laboratories in the United States are public, meaning they receive their money from and are operated by a federal, state, or local unit of government. Somewhere around 470 of these are in operation today. Some 30 to 50 private forensic science laboratories are also in operation.

Public Forensic Science Laboratories

Public forensic science laboratories are financed and operated by a unit of government. Different jurisdictions have different models for where the laboratory appears in the governmental hierarchy. Federal laboratories have their own positions within the federal system.

Federal Government Forensic Science Laboratories

The federal forensic science laboratory that most people are familiar with is the Federal Bureau of Investigation (FBI) Laboratory. This is arguably the most famous forensic science laboratory in the world but it is hardly the only federal forensic laboratory.

The Department of Justice

The Federal Bureau of Investigation (FBI) is a unit of the Department of Justice. It has one operational laboratory and a research center (Forensic Science Research and Training Center) near their Training Academy in Quantico, Virginia. The FBI Laboratory assists the investigations of its own Special Agents. The FBI Laboratory will, upon request, analyze evidence that has not already been examined by any duly authorized law enforcement agency or forensic science laboratory. As one of the largest and most comprehensive forensic laboratories in the world, the FBI Laboratory provides analyses of physical evidence ranging from blood and other biological materials to explosives, drugs, and firearms. More than one million examinations are conducted by the FBI laboratory every year.

The Drug Enforcement Administration (DEA) is responsible for investigating major criminal drug operations and to help prevent drugs from other countries entering the United States. The DEA has a network of seven drug laboratories throughout the United States: Washington, DC; Miami, FL; Chicago, IL; Dallas, TX; San Francisco, CA; New York City, NY: and San Diego, CA. They also maintain a research laboratory, the Special Testing and Research Laboratory, in Chantilly, VA. The DEA Laboratories also support investigations with local or regional law enforcement as well as in joint operations.

The Department of the Treasury

If someone says "treasury," "money" is the first thing that probably comes to mind but the Treasury Department has several forensic science laboratories that analyze a full range of evidence. ATF's laboratory system is composed of the National Laboratory Center (NLC) in Rockville, Maryland, and the regional laboratories in Atlanta, Georgia, and San Francisco, California. The NLC is the second-oldest Federal laboratory in the United States. In addition, ATF's laboratories hold the distinction of being the first Federal laboratory system accredited by the American Society of Crime Laboratory Directors. These multidisciplined laboratories support the Bureau's explosives and arson programs. The laboratories routinely examine arson debris to detect accelerants, as well as intact and functioned explosive devices and explosives debris to identify device components and the explosives used. The laboratories also provide trace evidence comparisons. A new Fire Research Laboratory, the largest of its kind in the world, was built in conjunction with the Rockville laboratory. The name of the agency would seem to indicate what it analyzes—alcohol, tobacco and firearms—but the ATF laboratories also are renowned for their expertise in fire scene analysis and explosives. ATF has enhanced its analytical offerings and now offers a nearly full range of forensic services.

The United States Secret Service Laboratory in Washington, DC, has two main functions. First, forensic examiners in the Forensic Services Division (FSD) provide analysis for questioned documents, fingerprints, false identification, credit cards, and other related forensic science areas. FSD also manages the Secret Service's polygraph program nationwide. The division coordinates photographic, graphic, video, and audio, and image enhancement service, as well as the Voice Identification Program. Much of the forensic assistance the Secret Service offers is unique technology operated in this country only by FSD. The FSD Laboratory has one of the world's largest libraries of ink standards and questioned document analysis is one of their primary functions. The other function is in support of the Secret Service's role in executive protection. The laboratory researches and develops countermeasures and technologies for the protection of the president and other officials. As part of the 1994 Crime Bill, Congress mandated the Secret Service to provide forensic/technical assistance in matters involving missing and sexually exploited children. FSD offers this assistance to federal, state, and local law enforcement agencies, the Morgan P. Hardiman Task Force, and the National Center for Missing and Exploited Children (NCMEC).

Another agency that may not be associated normally with a forensic laboratory is the Internal Revenue Service (IRS) which has a laboratory in Chicago, IL. The IRS Laboratory specializes in questioned document analysis, especially inks and papers. Authentication of signatures on tax returns, fraudulent documentation relating to taxation, and other forms of fraud with the aim of avoiding federal taxes are their bread and butter.

The Department of the Interior

The U.S. Fish and Wildlife Service (USFWS) operates a unique forensic science laboratory in Ashland, OR. The USFWS Laboratory performs animal-oriented forensic analyses and its mission is to support the efforts of the Service's investigators who patrol the National Parks. The Laboratory supports the FWS Agents in their investigations of poachers and people who kill or injure endangered species. The Laboratory examines evidence involving animals and has specialized expertise in the identification of hooves, hairs, feathers, bone, and other animal tissues. It works with similar investigative agencies from other countries to track poachers and people who traffic in animal parts, such as bear gall bladders (in Asia, bear gall is thought to improve sexual potency) and elephant ivory. The USFWS Laboratory is a sophisticated facility that has some of the world's leading experts in animal forensic science.

The U.S. Postal Service

While the U.S. Postal Service is not strictly a federal agency, it is considered to be a quasi-federal agency. The Postal Service has a laboratory in the Washington, DC, area that supports the Service's efforts to combat postal fraud. It does this through the analysis of questioned document, fingerprints, and trace evidence (hairs, fibers, particles, etc.).

State and Local Forensic Science Laboratories

Every state in the United States has at least one forensic science laboratory. State forensic science laboratories traditionally are housed in one of two places: Law enforcement or health departments. Law enforcement is used most often. The bulk of nonfederal public forensic laboratories is a part of a state or local law enforcement agency. The remainder is located in health departments or some other scientific agency within the governmental hierarchy. In all states there is a statewide laboratory or laboratory system that is operated by the state police or the state department of justice. Some states' laboratories are independent of the state law enforcement system, such as in Virginia. In California, for example, the state department of justice operates an extensive network of state-financed laboratories whereas West Virginia has a single laboratory that serves the whole state.

Most states also have laboratories operated by a local governmental unit, such as a large city or county. For example, in Maryland some counties have laboratories under the jurisdiction of the county police department separate from the state system. In California, Los Angeles has a county laboratory that has some overlapping jurisdiction with the city laboratory. In Michigan, the Detroit City Police Department has its own forensic science laboratory but the rest of Wayne County surrounding Detroit is serviced by the state police laboratories. This confusing hodge-podge of politics and geography may seem wasteful but has developed because of real societal needs, such as population levels, crime rates, and economics.

Private Forensic Science Laboratories

Private forensic laboratories typically perform only one or two types of examinations, such as drug analysis, toxicology, or DNA (Deoxyribonucleic acid). Some "laboratories" are a retired forensic scientist providing examinations in the specialties he or she performed when they were employed in a public forensic laboratory. A significant number of the (larger) private forensic laboratories are dedicated to DNA analysis; many of these also perform paternity testing (determining who the parents, usually the father, are). These private laboratories serve a needed function in the criminal justice system because they provide forensic services directly to persons involved or interested in crimes, that is, the suspects or defendants. Public forensic laboratories work only on those cases submitted by police or other duly authorized law enforcement offices (Office of the State Attorney or Office of the Chief Medical Examiner, for example). They will not—and usually cannot—analyze evidence submitted by anyone else except as ordered by a judge or other appropriate official. Some public forensic laboratories will accept evidence from private citizens, however, and the fee or cost is subsidized by the jurisdiction (city, county, and municipality) where the laboratory operates.

Forensic Science Laboratory Services

Not all forensic science laboratories offer the same types of analyses. In a state laboratory system, for example, typically one laboratory will offer a full range of forensic science services and the regional laboratories provide limited services (e.g., fingerprints, firearms, and drug analysis). It is important to note that "full service" does not always mean "every service"—a laboratory may not analyze gunshot residue analysis and still describe itself as "full service."

A recent National Institute of Justice (NIJ) publication of census data of forensic laboratories from 2002 demonstrate the variability of services offered (figure 1.1).

Evidence Control and Intake

Receiving, managing, and returning evidence is a central function of any forensic science laboratory. In a small laboratory, one employee may be assigned to fulfill this function while in a larger one, several people may work in an Evidence Unit. The evidence must be stored in a secured area to ensure its integrity; depending on the amount of casework, this

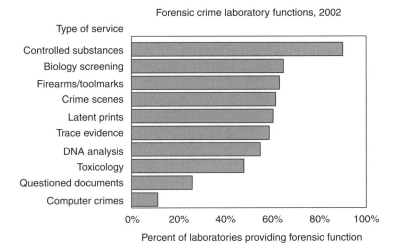

Figure 1.1 diagram: "Forensic crime laboratory functions, 2002" — horizontal bar chart. Type of service (vertical axis): Controlled substances, Biology screening, Firearms/toolmarks, Crime scenes, Latent prints, Trace evidence, DNA analysis, Toxicology, Questioned documents, Computer crimes. Horizontal axis: Percent of laboratories providing forensic function (0% to 100%).

Figure 1.1   Not all forensic laboratories conduct all analyses
Source: Bureau of Justice Statistics Bulletin, NCJ 207205, February 2005

area may be a room or an entire building. Evidence is submitted by a police officer or investigator who fills out paperwork describing the evidence and the type of examinations requested. The laboratory will assign a unique laboratory number to the case—in modern laboratories, this is done through a computerized Laboratory Information Management System (LIMS). Each item of evidence is labeled with the unique laboratory number, along with other identifying information, such as the item number. The documentation of the location of evidence from the time it is collected at the crime scene until it is presented in court is called the chain of custody. When evidence is transferred from one scientist to another, the first scientist lists the items to be transferred, prints his or her name, writes the date and time of the transfer, and signs the form. The person receiving the evidence prints their name and also signs the form; the chain of custody form permanently accompanies the laboratory case file. Just as a business must have a system of inventory control to know what goods they have and how much they have sold, so too must a forensic science laboratory have a system for inventorying evidence.

LIMS uses computerized systems that help laboratories keep track of evidence and information about analyses. Think of them as databases that generate labels, barcodes, or other tags to identify and inventory evidence. This automation greatly assists large laboratories where perhaps tens of thousands of evidence items flow through the facility each year—the FBI Laboratory, for example, performs over 2 million examinations per year.

Analytical Sections

Evidence from a case is assigned to one or more forensic units within the laboratory for analysis. Each unit then assigns an individual scientist to be responsible for the evidence and its analysis. Several scientists may be assigned to the same case, each responsible for their own specific analyses (DNA, fingerprints, firearms, etc.). Conversely, one item of evidence may be analyzed by several scientists in turn. Take the example of a threatening letter, one that allegedly contains anthrax or some other contagious material. The envelope and the letter could be subjected to the following exams, in order:

- Disease diagnosis, to determine whether it really contains the suspected contagion
- Trace evidence, for hairs or fibers in the envelope or stuck to the adhesives (stamp, closure, tape used to seal it)
- DNA, from saliva on the stamp or the envelope closure
- Questioned documents, for the paper, lettering, and other aspects of the form of the letter
- Ink analysis, to determine what was used to write the message, address, and so on.
- Handwriting, typewriter, or printer analysis, as appropriate
- Latent fingerprints
- Content analysis, to evaluate the nature of the writer's intent and other investigative clues

The order of the exams is important: the first scientist does not want to destroy the evidence the next scientist needs to analyze. As an example, a full service laboratory analytical sections might contain the following sections:

- Photography
- Biology/DNA
- Firearms and Tool marks
- Footwear and Tire Treads
- Questioned Documents
- Friction Ridge Analysis
- Chemistry/Illegal Drugs
- Toxicology
- Trace Evidence

The term "trace evidence" is specific to forensic science; it may also be called "criminalistics," "microchemistry," or "microanalysis." This area generally encompasses the analysis of hairs, fibers, soils, glass, paints, plastics, ignitable liquids, explosives, building materials, inks, and dyes. The common link between all these evidence materials is that they often appear as small pieces of the original source. Therefore, a microscope is used to examine and analyze them. The microscope may be integrated into another scientific instrument so that the very small samples can be analyzed.

The term "criminalistics" is sometimes used to describe certain areas of forensic science. Criminalistics is a word imported into English from the German *kriminalistik*. The word was coined to capture the various aspects of applying scientific and technological methods to the investigation and resolution of legal matters. In California and western states in the United States, forensic scientists working in forensic science laboratories may call themselves "criminalists." Criminalistics is generally thought of as the branch of forensic science that involves collection and analysis of physical evidence generated by criminal activity. It includes areas such as drugs, firearms and tool marks, fingerprints, blood and body fluids, footwear, and trace evidence. Trace evidence is a term of art that means different things to different people. It might include fire and explosive residues, glass, soils, hairs, fibers, paints, plastics and other polymers, wood, metals, and chemicals.

Other Laboratory Services

Sometimes forensic laboratories offer services other than those listed above, such as blood stain pattern analysis, entomology, anthropology, or other specialties. For smaller laboratories that have only an occasional need for these services may submit the evidence to the FBI laboratory, a private laboratory, or a local specialist.

Specialty Areas of Forensic Science

Forensic Pathology

Back in the days when the Quincy television show was popular, many people thought of forensic pathology and forensic science as the same thing—this misperception persists even today. The forensic pathologist is a medical doctor, specially trained in clinical and anatomic pathology

(pathology is the study of diseases and trauma), whose function is to determine the cause and manner of death in cases where the death occurred under suspicious or unknown circumstances. This often involves a teamwork approach with the autopsy or postmortem examination of the body as the central function. Forensic pathologists or their investigators are often called to death scenes to make some preliminary observations including an estimate of the time since death.

Forensic Anthropology

Forensic anthropology is a branch of physical anthropology, the study of humans, their biology, and their ancestors. Forensic anthropology deals with identifying people who cannot be identified through fingerprints, photographs, or other similar means. Typically, forensic anthropologists analyze skeletal remains to determine whether they are human and, if they are, the age, sex, height, and other characteristics of the deceased are also analyzed. Forensic anthropologists are central to the reconstruction and identification of victims in mass fatalities, such as bombings and airplane crashes. Working closely with pathologists, dentists, and others, forensic anthropologists aid in the identification of victims who otherwise might not be found.

Forensic Dentistry

Sometimes called forensic odontology, forensic dentistry serves a number of purposes to the forensic sciences. These include identification of human remains in mass disasters (the enamel in teeth is the hardest material produced by the body and intact teeth are often found at disaster sites), post mortem x-rays of the teeth can be compared to antemortem x-rays, and the comparison of bitemarks.

Forensic Engineering

Forensic engineers analyze why things fail—everything from faulty toasters that electrocute people to buildings and bridges that crumble apart and kill many people. For example, forensic engineering assisted greatly in the analysis of the September 11 attacks on the World Trade Center and the Pentagon. Forensic engineers may also help to reconstruct traffic accidents. Based on tire skid marks, damage to vehicles and surrounding items, and the laws of physics, they can determine path, direction, speed, and the type of collision that occurred.

Toxicology

Toxicologists analyze body fluids and tissues to determine whether toxic substances, such as drugs or poisons, are present. If they identify such a substance, they then determine how much is present and what effect, if any, the substance might have had to impair, hurt, or kill the person. Forensic toxicologists work closely with forensic pathologists. Many of the cases forensic toxicologists work involve drunk driving, or operating under the influence, as well as determination of the blood or breath for alcohol content.

Behavioral Sciences

Popularized by television programs, such as Profiler, and movies, such as *Silence of the Lambs*, forensic psychiatrists and psychologists do not only hunt serial killers. They also determine a person's competency to stand trial and aiding in one's own defense, study developmental and mental causes of an individual's criminal activity, and counsel victims. Competency to stand trial is a recurring issue because insanity has been a common legal defense. To complicate things, each state has its own standards for what constitutes insanity. The central question is whether or not the defendant was in a mental capacity to know right actions from wrong ones. Behavioral forensic scientists also assist investigations of serial crimes by creating psychological profiles of the criminals. People tend to act in predictable patterns when they commit crimes and the discovery of these behavioral patterns can provide clues to the personality of the offender. Behavioral scientists may also be called upon to help in interviewing or interrogating suspects in crimes. Although profiling can provide useful information about who the police should look for, it is not an exact science by any means.

Questioned Documents

A questioned document is just that—a document whose authenticity is in question. The examination of questioned documents (or "QD") is a complicated and wide-ranging area of study often requiring a great deal of study, mentoring, and training. QD Examiners may be required to analyze any or all of the following: Handwriting, typewriting, printed documents, inks, or paper to determine the source or authenticity of a particular document. Documents also may be examined to detect erasures, obliterations, forgeries, alterations, and counterfeiting (mostly currency).

Professional Organizations

Professional organizations cater to specific subgroups within forensic science, such as document examiners, medical examiners, fingerprint examiners, and so on.. The major professional organizations are listed below (alphabetically) with their websites.*

American Academy of Forensic Sciences	www.aafs.org
American Society of Crime Laboratory Directors	www.ascld.org
Association of Forensic Quality Assurance Managers	www.afquam.org
California Association of Criminalists	www.cac.org
International Association for Identification	www.theiai.org
Mid-Atlantic Association of Forensic Sciences	www.maafs.org
Midwest Association of Forensic Sciences	www.mafs.org
National Association of Medical Examiners	www.thename.org
Northeastern Association of Forensic Sciences	www.neafs.org
Northwestern Association of Forensic Sciences	www.nwafs.org
Society of Forensic Toxicologists	www.soft.org
Southern Association of Forensic Sciences	www.safs.org
Southwestern Association of Forensic Sciences	www.swafs.org

These professional organizations meet, sometimes multiple times, around the United States to present research results, share information, and learn from colleagues. Many of these organizations have student membership status and all of them provide additional information about their areas of interest on their websites.

Accreditation, Standardization, and Certification

Accreditation is the process by which a laboratory guarantees that its services are offered with a certain degree of quality, integrity, and assurance. The accreditation process is extensive, rigorous, and demanding for the laboratory that undertakes it. The laboratory and its staff first undergo a comprehensive self-study with a long checklist of requirements. The laboratory then applies for accreditation. The accrediting agency sends out a team to perform an on-site evaluation by trained members of the

* Websites change regularly; it may be necessary to use a search engine to locate a website.

accrediting board. If the laboratory passes the evaluation, it becomes accredited. It is important to remember that accreditation says nothing about the competence of the individual forensic scientists who work at the laboratory. That would be called certification. Being accredited does mean that the laboratory meets certain minimum criteria for the facilities, security, training, equipment, quality assurance and control, and other essentials. In the United States, forensic science laboratories can be accredited through two agencies. The first is the American Society of Crime Laboratory Directors (ASCLD) Laboratory Accreditation Board (ASCLD-LAB). ASCLD is a professional organization of forensic science laboratory directors; ASCLD-LAB is a separate but related organization. Reaccreditation is required every five years in order to maintain the laboratory's status. Forensic laboratories can also seek accreditation through the International Standards Organization (ISO) under its 17025 standard. As part of its long-term plan, ASCLD-LAB is transitioning to the ISO platform.

Standards play a major role in helping laboratories become accredited. A standard can take two forms. It can be a written standard, which is like a very specific recipe, and has to be followed exactly to get the proper result. The ASTM, International (American Society for Testing and Materials, International) publishes standards for a wide variety of sciences, including forensic science (in Volume 14.02). These standards are written by groups of experts in the field who come to agreement on the acceptable way to perform a certain analysis. A standard can also be a physical thing, such as a sample of pure copper. Physical standards such as this are called reference materials because scientists refer to them when analyzing other samples. If a specimen is 99.999% pure copper, its properties are known exactly, as for example, how it ought to react in an experiment. If the reference material has been tested extensively by many methods, it can be issued as a certified reference material (CRM). CRMs come with certificates guaranteeing their purity or quality. The National Institute of Standards and Technology (NIST) is the main agency of the U.S. government that issues CRMs.

Education and Training of Forensic Scientists

Science is the heart of forensic science. Court decisions, such as *Daubert v. Merrill Dow*,[1] have reinforced that a forensic scientist must be well versed in the methods and requirements of good science in general and in the specific techniques used in the particular disciplines being practiced. Additionally, the forensic scientist must be familiar with the rules of evidence and court procedures in the relevant jurisdictions. The knowledge, skills, and aptitudes needed in these areas are gained by a combination of formal education, formal training, and experience.

Historically, forensic scientists were recruited from the ranks of university chemistry or biology department graduates. Little or no education was provided in the forensic sciences themselves; all of the forensic stuff was learned on the job. For many years, forensic science has been offered only by a handful of colleges and universities in the United States. The popularity of forensic science has caused an explosion in forensic-oriented programs and students interested in a forensic career. Many of these programs offered weak curricula, little science, and had no faculty with forensic experience. This created applicants who lacked the necessary education and skills for the laboratory positions. *Forensic Science: Review of Status and Needs*, a published report from the National Institute of Justice (NIJ) in 1999,[2] noted that the educational and training needs

> of the forensic community are immense. Training of newcomers to the field, as well as providing continuing education for seasoned professionals, is vital to ensuring that crime laboratories deliver the best possible service to the criminal justice system. Forensic scientists must stay up to date as new technology, equipment, methods, and techniques are developed. While training programs exist in a variety of forms, there is need to broaden their scope and build on existing resources.

Forensic Science: Review of Status and Needs made a number of recommendations, including seeking mechanisms for

- accreditation/certification of forensic academic training programs/ institutions;
- setting national consensus standards of education in the forensic sciences;
- ensuring that all forensic scientists have professional orientations to the field; formal quality-assurance training, and expert witness training.

The Technical Working Group on Education and Training in Forensic Science (TWGED) was created in response to the needs expressed by the justice system, including the forensic science and law enforcement communities, to establish models for training and education in forensic science. West Virginia University, in conjunction with the National Institute of Justice, sponsored TWGED which was made up of over 50 forensic scientists, educators, laboratory directors, and professionals. TWGED drafted a guide addressing qualifications for a career in forensic science, undergraduate curriculum in forensic science, graduate education in forensic science, training and continuing education, and forensic science careers outside of the traditional forensic science laboratory.

Seeing this as an opportunity, the American Academy of Forensic Sciences (AAFS) initiated the Forensic Science Education Program Accreditation Commission (FEPAC) as a standing committee of the Academy. The FEPAC drafted accreditation standards for forensic education programs based on the TWGED guidelines. The mission of the FEPAC is to maintain and to enhance the quality of forensic science education through a formal evaluation and recognition of college-level academic programs. The primary function of the Commission is to develop and to maintain standards and to administer an accreditation program that recognizes and distinguishes high quality undergraduate and graduate forensic science programs. The work of FEPAC has made it easier for students and laboratory directors to evaluate forensic educational programs.

Educational programs are not, however, designed up to provide training so that a graduate can start working cases on their first day in a forensic science laboratory. Once a scientist is employed by a forensic science laboratory, they begin formal training. New scientists are normally hired as specialists—they will learn how to analyze evidence in one or a group of related areas. Thus, someone may be hired as a drug analyst, a trace evidence analyst, or a firearms examiner. Training requires a period of apprenticeship where the newly hired scientist works closely with an experienced scientist. The length of time for training varies widely with the discipline and the laboratory. For example, a drug chemist may train for three to six months before taking cases, while a DNA analyst may train for one to two years, and a questioned document examiner may spend up to three years in apprenticeship. Time and resource management skills develop and the pressure of testifying in court hones your abilities. Learning how to "hurry up and wait" to testify, how to handle the media (or not), and how to deal with harried attorneys are all part of a forensic scientist's growth. These are aspects of the career that are difficult to convey to someone who has not experienced them.

History and Pioneers

Early examples of what we would now call forensic science are scattered throughout history. In an ancient Chinese text, "The Washing Away of Wrongs," from the thirteenth century, the first recorded forensic entomology case is mentioned. A man was stabbed near a rice field and the investigating magistrate came to the scene the following day. He told the field hands to lay down their sickles, used to cut the rice stalks, on the floor in front of them. Blow flies, which are attracted to rotting flesh, were drawn to tiny traces of blood on one of the sickles—but to none of the others. The owner of that sickle was confronted and he ultimately confessed.

Forensic science emerged during the nineteenth century at time when many factors were influencing society. European and American cities were growing in size and complexity. People who were used to knowing everyone in their neighborhood or village were increasingly encountering new and different people. Transients and crooks, traveled from city to city, committing crimes and becoming invisible in the crowds. Repeat criminal offenders who wanted to escape the law had only to move to a new town, give a false name, and no one would be the wiser. It became important for government to be able to identify citizens because it might not be able to trust them to provide their true identity.

Fictional Pioneers

In this shifting society, the fictional detective story was born. Acting as loners, working with but outside of the established police force, these literary characters helped to define what would become forensic science. One of the first of these "fictional pioneers" was a 32-year-old assistant editor in Richmond, Virginia.

Edgar Allan Poe

Born in Boston on January 19, 1809, Edgar Allan Poe became the father of the modern American mystery story. He was educated in Virginia and England as a child. Poe worked for several publications as both editor and writer, his success as the former coinciding with his growth as the latter. His early work was highly praised but did not create enough income for him and his wife to live on. His reputation did help sales, however, as did macabre tales of suspense such as "The Fall of the House of Usher." Poe published other trademark tales of horror, such as "The Tell-Tale Heart," and "The Pit and The Pendulum." His haunting poem, "The Raven," published in 1845, assured Poe of literary fame.

Mystery and crime stories as they appear today did not emerge until Poe introduced mystery fiction's first fictional detective, Auguste C. Dupin, in the 1841 story, "The Murders in the Rue Morgue."

Poe continued Dupin's exploits in novels such as *The Mystery of Marie Roget* (1842) and *The Purloined Letter* (1845). Dupin is a man of singular intelligence and logical thinking. His powers of observation are acute and seemingly superhuman. Dupin's conclusions are not pure logic; there is a good amount of intuition and "educated guessing" in his mental gymnastics. A hallmark of later fictional—and real—detectives, creativity is central to good sleuthing.

Dupin and his nameless narrator read of the horrible murder of a woman and her daughter in their apartment on the Rue Morgue. The bodies have been mutilated and the apartment torn to shreds. Neighbors talk of a foreigner speaking in a guttural language no one understands. Dupin comments to his companion on the sensationalism of the newspaper story and the ineptness of the police.

> They have fallen into the gross but common error of confounding the unusual with the abstruse. But it is by these deviations from the plane of the ordinary, that reason feels its way, if at all, in its search for the true. In investigations such as we are now pursuing, it should not be so much asked "what has occurred," as "what has occurred that has never occurred before." In fact, the facility with which I shall arrive, or have arrived, at the solution of this mystery, is in the direct ration of its apparent insolubility in the eyes of the police.[3]

The amateur detectives secure the permission of the Prefect of the Police (equivalent to the Chief of a modern day police force) to assist in the investigation. Although they assist the police, Dupin is critical of their methods.

> The Parisian police, so much extolled for acumen, are cunning, but no more. There is no method in their proceedings, beyond the method of the moment. They make a vast parade of measures; but, not infrequently, these are . . . ill-adapted to the objects proposed. . . . The results attained by them are not infrequently surprising, but for the most part, are brought about by simple diligence and activity. . . . Thus there is such a thing as being too profound.[4]

Real detectives of the time did employ "simple diligence and activity" in their investigations, what Colin Wilson has termed "the needle-in-a-haystack" method.[5] They had little knowledge of forensic evidence as detectives do today and slogged along doggedly in pursuit of the slightest clue. Poe's detective goes on to solve the case in a style that sets the stage for fictional detectives for decades to come.

A famous case during Poe's lifetime illustrates the "needle-in-a-haystack" method. The double murder of the Chardon family was discovered a week and a half before Christmas in 1834. A widow and her son were found brutally murdered in their Paris home: She was stabbed to death and he had his head cut open by a hatchet. Initial suspicion fell upon the son's acquaintances but the case turned cold. On New Year's Eve, the attempted murder of a bank courier was reported. The courier had been sent to collect funds from a man named Mahossier. The courier found the address, knocked, and entered. The young man was grabbed from behind and stabbed in the back. But he managed to wrestle free from his attacker and cry for help. His attacker fled.

The Sûreté, Paris' counterpart of London's Scotland Yard, assigned the same detective, named Canler, to both cases. Canler did what detectives did in those days—he began a search of every low-rent hotel and rooming house in Paris for a guest register with the name "Mahossier." He found a hotel that had registered a Mahossier but the proprietors could not provide a description. Inquiring about the guest just below Mahossier—named François—Canler heard a description that reminded him of a criminal who had just been jailed. Canler interrogated François and found that he knew Mahossier and had helped him with the attempt on the bank courier's life. However, he did not know his real name. Back to the streets went Canler. He visited the usual criminal hang-outs and shopped the description of Mahossier only to find out his real name was Gaillard. Canler found poetry and letters in another hotel room and compared it with the handwriting of Mahossier; they were the same.

Meantime, François had been to trial and was convicted. Canler decided to visit François on his way to prison. Desperate to make good somehow, François told Canler he could help him with the Chardon killings. He had been drinking with a man who claimed to be the Chardons' killer while another man kept watch. The killer said his name was *Gaillard*. Gaillard's accomplice in the Chardon case was another prisoner who confessed once he was confronted with Gaillard's murderous nature. The man told Canler of Gaillard's aunt and where she lived. Canler visited the aunt who told police she feared for her life from her nephew. His real name? Pierre-François-Lacenaire. As will be seen later, this is why it was so difficult for police to track criminals in the days before our modern electronic communications were invented. A warrant went out for Lacenaire's arrest.

At the beginning of February, Canler received notice that Lacenaire had been arrested for passing forged money in another town. A canny understanding of the criminal psyche led Canler to suggest to Lacenaire that his accomplices had implicated him in his crimes. Lacenaire refused to believe his accomplices would "squeal" on him; in prison, however, he asked around whether that was true. Friends of François took poorly to the impugning of their fellow criminal and beat Lacenaire mercilessly. When he was released from the prison hospital, he confessed his crimes to Canler and implicated both his accomplices. Lacenaire was executed a year later, in January 1835. This case demonstrates the criminal investigative methodology in place in the early 1800s—dogged, persistent searching. Little to no physical evidence was used because the police disregarded it as "circumstantial"; that is, abstract and removed from their daily work. The pioneering successes of early forensic scientists in the late 1800s changed all that and increasingly brought science into investigations and the courtroom.

Arthur Conan Doyle

Born in Edinburgh, Scotland, in 1859, Arthur Conan Doyle studied to be a doctor at the University of Edinburgh. While at medical school, Doyle had been greatly inspired by one of his professors, John Bell. Bell displayed an uncanny deductive reasoning to diagnose diseases. After he graduated, Doyle set up a small medical practice at Southsea in Hampshire. He was not entirely successful as a medical doctor but his lack of patients gave him time to write. Doyle had been so influenced by Bell that he incorporated his ideas and patterns of thinking in his most famous character. Sherlock Holmes was introduced in *A Study in Scarlet* (1887), and reappeared in *A Sign of Four* in 1890. It was not until *Strand* magazine published a series of stories called "The Adventures of Sherlock Holmes" that Holmes became popular. An instant hit, the public clamored for more stories of the Consulting Detective and Dr. John H. Watson, his friend and confidant.

From 1891 to 1893, *Strand* published stories featuring Holmes and Watson, all avidly followed by the public. Doyle became weary of writing the detective stories and decided to end his character's career. In *The Final Problem* (1893), Holmes and his longtime arch enemy, Professor James Moriarty, killed each other in a battle at Reichenbach Falls. The public rebelled and Doyle was forced to bring Holmes back from the dead. Holmes and Watson continued their adventures in *The Hound of the*

Baskervilles (1902). More books and stories were published until *The Case-Book of Sherlock Holmes* appeared in 1927. Doyle died in 1930. In all, Holmes and Watson were featured in 4 novels and 56 stories.

Like Dupin, Holmes possessed superior intelligence, keen observation skills, and dogged persistence. These are the hallmarks of fictional detectives. Real forensic investigators use intuition and deduction as well. Holmes' unique trait was the use of science in his investigations. Doyle presaged many uses and methods employed routinely by forensic detectives in later years; blood typing and microscopy are well-known examples.

Pioneers in Forensic Science

Francois Quetelet

A gifted Belgian mathematician and astronomer, Francois Quetelet (1796–1874) applied statistical reasoning to social phenomena, something that had not been done before. His work profoundly influenced the European social sciences. The history of the social sciences from the late 1830s onwards is, in large measure, the story of the application and refinement of ideas about the operation of probability in human affairs. These ideas about probability gained widespread currency in intellectual and government circles through the writings of Quetelet. Quetelet's life-long interest in gathering and interpreting statistics began in earnest in the early 1820s, when he was employed by the government of the Low Countries to improve the collection and interpretation of census data. European governments had made practical use of probability well before the 1820s; however, Quetelet was convinced that probability influenced the course of human affairs more profoundly than his contemporaries appreciated.

Quetelet was born in Ghent, Belgium on February 22, 1796. He received a doctorate of science in 1819 from the University of Ghent. He taught mathematics in Brussels after 1819 and founded and directed the Royal Observatory. Quetelet had studied astronomy and probability for three months in Paris in 1824. He learned astronomy from Arago and Bouvard and the theory of probability from Joseph Fourier and Pierre Laplace. He learned how to run the observatory. And Quetelet gave special attention to the meteorological functions of the observatory.

One science was not enough, however, for Quetelet. Starting around 1830, he became heavily involved in statistics and sociology. Quetelet was convinced that probability influenced the course of human affairs more than other scientists of his time thought it did. Astronomers had used the law of error to gain accurate measurement of phenomena in the physical world. Quetelet believed the law of error could be applied to human beings also. If the phenomena analyzed were part of human nature, Quetelet believed that it was possible to determine the average physical and intellectual features of a population. Through gathering the "facts of life," the behavior of individuals could be assessed against how an "average man" would normally behave. Quetelet believed it was possible to identify the underlying regularities for both normal and abnormal behavior. The "average man" could be known from statistically arraying the facts of life and analyzing the results.

Quetelet had come to be known as the champion of a new science, dedicated to mapping the normal physical and moral characteristics of societies through statistics: Quetelet called it social mechanics. His most influential book was *Sur l'homme et le développement de se facultés, ou Essai de physique sociale* (*A Treatise on Man, and the Development of His Faculties*), published in 1835. In it, he outlines the project of a social physics and describes his concept of the "average man" (*l'homme moyen*) who is characterized by the mean values of measured variables that follow a normal distribution. He collected data about many such variables. Quetelet thought more of "average" physical and mental qualities as real properties of particular people or races and not just abstract concepts. Quetelet helped give cognitive strength to ideas of racial differences in nineteenth-century European thought. Quetelet's concept of "average man" is that it is the central value around which measurements of a human trait are grouped according to a normal bell curve. The "average man" began as a simple way of summarizing some characteristic of a population, but in some of Quetelet's later work, he presents "average man" as an ideal type. He felt that nature intended the "average man" as a goal and any deviations from this goal were errors or aberrations. These later ideas were criticized by other scientists—they argued that an average for a population in all dimensions might not even be biologically feasible. What Quetelet thought he was measuring might not even exist, in his critics' view.

In 1846, he published a book on probability and social science that contained a diverse collection of human measurements, such as the heights of men conscripted into the French military and the chest circumferences of Scottish soldiers. The data were in many cases approximately normally distributed. Quetelet was among the first who attempted to apply it to social science, planning what he called a "social physics." He was keenly aware of the overwhelming complexity of social phenomena, and the many variables that needed measurement. His goal was to understand the statistical laws underlying such phenomena as crime rates, marriage rates or suicide rates. He wanted to explain the values of these variables by other social factors. The use of the normal curve, a standard in many sciences such as astronomy but not in the social sciences, in this way had a powerful influence on other scientists, such as Francis Galton and James Clark Maxwell. His study of the statistics of crime and its implications for the populations and races under study prompted questions of free will versus social determinism. These ideas were rather controversial at the time among other scientists who held that it contradicted a concept of freedom of choice. Were criminals born or made? Were certain populations destined to be criminals or could people choose to lead an honest life? Quetelet's work on the statistics of crime and mortality was used by the government to improve census taking and make policy decisions on issues, such as immigration, policing, and welfare.

Quetelet also founded several statistical journals and societies, and was especially interested in creating international cooperation among statisticians. He influenced generations of social scientists who studied statistics, populations, races, and crime.

Caesare Lombroso

During the later part of the nineteenth century, Caesare Lombroso (1835–1909), an Italian physician who worked in prisons, suggested that criminals have distinctive physical traits. He viewed them as evidence of evolutionary regression to lower forms of human or animal life. To Lombroso, a criminals' "degenerate" physical appearance reflected their degenerate mental state—which led them to commit crimes. In 1876, Lombroso theorized that criminals stand out physically, with low foreheads, prominent jaws and cheekbones, protruding ears, hairiness, and unusually long arms. Lombroso felt that all these characteristics made them look like humans' apelike ancestors who were not as developed as modern humans and, therefore, made criminals lesser humans.

But Lombroso's work was flawed, since the physical features he attributed to prisoners could be found throughout the population. It is now known that no physical attributes, of the kind described by Lombroso, set off criminals from noncriminals.

Many criminals at the time were diagnosed with a disease called "dementia praecox," a disease that was considered practically incurable. The one who defined the diagnosis was the French psychiatrist Benedict Augustin Morel in 1860. Morel described a disorder where the intellectual faculties decompose to an apathetic state resembling dementia. Today, this would be recognized as a type of schizophrenia. Morel's work about the "degeneration" of the human species claimed that the disposition for mental diseases is passed through family generations and family members get increasingly more "degenerate" and mentally ill with each generation.

Ten years later, Lombroso adopted Morel's ideas but connected mental diseases and criminality. The ideas of Morel and Lombroso influenced many psychiatrists and academics. For example, the novel, *The Buddenbrooks* by Thomas Mann published in German in 1901, is about the decline and fall of a family due to mental illness. The ideas of mental degeneration due to family genetics exerted a disastrous influence on the later development of societies and politics in the United States and Europe, especially Germany.

His research was scientifically flawed. Several decades later, Charles Goring, a British psychiatrist, conducted a scientific comparison of prisoners and people living in the same society and found no overall physical differences. Today, genetics research seeks possible links between biology and crime. Though no conclusive evidence connects criminality to any specific genetic trait, people's overall genetic composition, in combination with social influences, probably accounts for some tendency toward criminality. In other words, biological factors may have a real, but modest, effect on whether or not an individual becomes a criminal.

Alphonse Bertillon (1853–1914)

By 1854, efforts were underway in police departments throughout Europe to create local archives of criminal images. The chief difficulty was how to identify habitual thieves (so-called "recidivists" or "career criminals," as they are called now). As cities grew and people became more mobile, knowing whether a person was really who they said they were became increasingly problematic. Judicial sentencing had changed to increase the severity of punishment based on the number and type of crimes committed. Therefore, the judges and the police had to know who the criminals were and whether they had a record of their past offences.

The photographs were an attempt to catalog recidivists. These included daguerreotype portraits of criminals and "rogues' galleries," which usually comprised photographs placed in racks or assembled into albums. Volumes of mug shots were compiled by local police agencies as well as by private detective organizations such as the Pinkerton National Detective Agency in the United States. Volumes containing records of illegal foreigners, for instance the itinerant Chinese population, were probably used for purposes of immigration control. From the 1880s on, identifying details and photographs were commonly featured in the "wanted" posters that were distributed widely to apprehend criminals.

The files developed contained the photographs and descriptions of criminals, which were typically of little use. It was not so much that the descriptions were not accurate—they were as far as that kind of thing goes—it was that there was no *system*. Imagine this: A police clerk has a criminal standing in front of him and the officer wants to know whether they had committed any crimes prior to the current one. The hundreds or possibly thousands of files must be sorted through in trying to recognize the face in front of the clerk from a photograph! Names are no good; the criminal might be lying. The files cannot be sorted by things such as beards because the criminal might have shaven to disguise his appearance. For any city of any size, this became an administrative nightmare. Now think of trying to communicate this information *between* towns and cities with no fax machines, no e-mail, and no Internet. Turning data into information is crucial when making sense of the data.

Policemen themselves began to include photographs in albums either for private record, as in the case of Jesse Brown Cook's scrapbooks, or to publicize police activity, as in Thomas Byrnes' *Professional Criminals of America* (1886). Byrnes' book reproduced photographs of mostly "respectable"-looking criminals with accompanying comments. Byrnes claimed that, contrary to popular opinion (because of Lombroso's work), criminals did not necessarily convey by their physical appearance the nature of their activities.

Alphonse Bertillon was the son of the anthropometrist Adolphe Louis Bertillon. Anthropometrics is the science of taxonomy of the human race, which relies on a statistical approach, using abstract measurements. Anthropometrics had been used extensively in the colonies by most European powers with colonial interests to study "primitive" peoples. It formed part of the foundation of the modern science of physical anthropology. Bertillon had always shown two traits that would define the rest of his life: Genius and rebelliousness. Alphonse had inherited his father's intelligence but it was tinged with an unwillingness to suffer those not as bright as he. Bertillon's father had tried to help him with employment but could not help him enough: Alphonse could only retain employment as a police clerk. The repetitive work of filling out and filing forms was mind-numbingly boring to him and he constantly searched for intellectual outlets.

Alphonse knew from the work of his father and Lombroso that people's characteristics could be measured and that criminals were physically different from "normal" people. Additionally, from the work of Quetelet, he knew that the measurements of human characteristics tend to fall into statistically relevant groups but also that no two people should have the same set of measurements. Bertillon surmised that if a record could be made of 11 special measurements of the human body, then that record, when accompanied with a photograph, would establish unique, recordable, systematized identification characteristics for every member of the human race.

Alphonse devised his method and wrote his ideas out as a proposal to the Prefect (Chief of Police). The Prefect, a good policeman with little formal education named Andrieux, promptly ignored it. Bertillon tried again with another report explaining his method. Andrieux became angry that this clerk was telling him the present system was useless and reprimanded him. Bertillon felt that he was condemned to fill out forms for the rest of his life. His father, however, counseled patience and to continue measuring anyone who would allow it and increase his data. Eventually, Andrieux was replaced by a man named Camecasse. Alphonse jumped at the chance and made his usual presentation. Camecasse was reluctant but gave Bertillon three months to identify at least one career criminal; if he could do that, his method would be adopted.

Bertillon had had two years under Andrieux to accumulate data and perfect his system. The Bertillonage measurements were:

1. Height
2. Stretch: Length of body from left shoulder to right middle finger when arm is raised
3. "Bust": Length of torso from head to seat, taken when seated
4. Length of head: Crown to forehead
5. Width of head: Temple to temple
6. Length of right ear
7. Length of left foot

8. Length of left middle finger
9. Length of left cubit: Elbow to tip of middle finger
10. Width of cheeks (presumably cheekbone)
11. Length of left little finger

These would be entered onto a data card, alongside the picture of the criminal, with additional information such as hair, beard, eye color and so on. Front view and profile photographs were taken (the precursor to our modern "mug shots"). Bertillon called these cards a *portrait parlé*, a spoken portrait that described the criminal both through measurements and words. This "Bertillon card" would then be filed in one of 81 drawers. The drawers were organized by length of head, then by width, then middle fingers, and finally little fingers. On these four measurements, Bertillon could get the odds of identifying any one criminal down to about 1 in 276. After that, the additional measurements would pin him down. The chances of two people having the same measurements were calculated at more than four million to one.

Two months and three weeks went by without a whiff of an identification. Bertillon was a nervous wreck. Near the end of the last week, Bertillon processed a criminal named Dupont (his sixth Dupont of the day, no less). After measuring Dupont, Bertillon sorted through his drawers and cards and found one that matched—the man's name was actually Martin. Bertillon went into the interrogation room and confronted the man with his real identity and arrest record. "Dupont" denied it but when Bertillon showed the arresting officer the photographs, clearing showing a mole the man had on his face, Martin finally confessed. Bertillon had done it!

Alphonse Bertillon eventually became Chief of Criminal Identification for the Paris Police. His system, named after him (Bertillonage), became recognized worldwide but was particularly popular in Europe, especially in France. Bertillon standardized the mug shot and the evidence picture and developed what he called *photographie métrique* (metric photography). Bertillon intended this system to enable its user to precisely reconstruct the dimension of a particular space and the placement of objects in it, or to measure the object represented. Such pictures documented a crime scene and the potential clues in it prior to its being disturbed in any way. Bertillon used special mats printed with *cadres métriques* (metric frames) which were mounted along the sides of these photographs. Included among these *photographies métriques* are those Bertillon called *photographies stéréometriques* (stereometric photographs), which pictured front and side views of a particular object.

Bertillon's system lasted approximately 20 years. It was abandoned for the same reason it became useful: The archive itself became unwieldy. The Bertillonage apparatus included an overhead camera, under which the subject would recline in the two poses for the measurement of stretch and height; plus a camera set up in precisely measured distance from the subject, for measurement of the facial dimensions, ear, torso, arm, and hand. All these images were photographed against a grided screen, so that the photographs could act as measurement records. Bertillon's equipment was standard photographic equipment with minor modifications. But the central instrument of the system was not the camera but the filing cabinet. At some point, it became too difficult to record, maintain, and search through tens of thousands of cards.

Beyond the complexity of the system, other issues began to undermine Bertillon's method. First, it was too difficult to get other clerks to collect measurements exactly in the way Bertillon wanted them taken. Bertillon was an exacting man and the difference between a couple of millimeters might keep a criminal from being identified. Second, a new forensic method was gaining ground that would overshadow Bertillonage: Fingerprints.

Hans Gross

Hans Gross (1847–1915) is generally acknowledged as the founder of scientific criminal investigation. His landmark book, *Handbuch fur Untersuchungsrichter* ("Handbook for Examining Magistrates," published in English as *Criminal Investigation*), published in 1893 placed science at the forefront of investigating criminal activities. Gross emphasized the use of the microscope in studying trace materials that might show associations between the criminal, the victim, and the crime scene. The handbook also included discussions of forensic medicine, toxicology, serology, and ballistics, as well as topics that had never been discussed before—physics, geology, and botany. Even in 1893, Gross complained about the lack of training and application of microscopy in the beginning of his chapter on that topic:

> Advanced though the construction of microscopes is today, and much as science can accomplish with this admirable artifact, the criminologist has as yet scarcely drawn upon the art of the microscopist. Studies of blood,

determination of semen spots, and comparison of hairs is virtually all that the microscopist has to do for the criminologist. Other investigations occur only exceptionally, although there are innumerable cases in which the microscopist could provide vital information and perhaps clarify insoluble problems.

Gross, his work, and his book went on to influence and inspire dozens of investigators and forensic scientists. The handbook has set the tone for forensic texts to this day.

Edmund Locard

The Paris police had been trying to track down a group of counterfeiters who were making false *franc* coins. Some of the alleged counterfeiters had been arrested but they refused to talk and reveal their sources. A young police scientist named Edmund Locard heard about the case and asked the inspector in charge to see the men's clothes. The inspector denied the request but Locard was persistent and repeated his request. Finally, the inspector gave Locard one set of clothing. Locard carefully brushed debris off the clothes, paying special attention to the sleeves and shirt cuffs. He then examined the debris under a microscope. Chemical analysis revealed the presence of tin, antimony, and lead—the exact components of the fake francs. The inspector was so impressed that he used Locard again; realizing his value in solving cases, other inspectors also caught on.

Locard was fascinated by the microscopic debris found on clothing and other items. He was inspired by the German chemist Liebig, who had contended, "Dust contains in small all the things that surround us." From his studies of microscopic materials, Locard knew that there was nothing organic or inorganic that would not eventually be broken, fractured, or splintered into dust or debris. This debris, indicative by shape, chemistry, or composition of its source, demonstrated the associations evident in our environments. He expounded on this concept:

> As a matter of fact, pulverization destroys the morphologic state which would enable us ordinarily to recognize these objects by our senses or even with our instruments. On the other hand, the transformation does not go so far to reduce the object into its ultimate elements, that is, into molecules or atoms. ([4], p. 279)

For example, cat or dog owners know it is not possible to leave the house without dog or cat hair on their clothing. A trained microscopist could determine:

- that they were hairs;
- in fact, animal hairs;
- specifically, dog or cat hairs;
- possibly identify the breed;
- and whether the hairs could have come from your dog or cat.

And it is that last part that creates the most value for criminal investigations. Demonstrating associations between people, places, and things involved in criminal acts is the focus of forensic science. Locard realized that the transfer and persistence of this debris was the key to unraveling the activities of criminals. In a paper he published in 1930, he stated,

> Yet, upon reflection, one is astonished that it has been necessary to wait until this late day for so simple an idea to be applied as the collecting, in the dust of garments, of the evidence of the objects rubbed against, and the contacts which a suspected person may have undergone. For the microscopic debris that cover our clothes and are the mute witnesses, sure and faithful, of all our movements and of all our encounters.

For years Locard studied the dust and debris from ordinary objects as well as evidence; he cataloged hundreds of samples. The amazing part is he did all this with a microscope, some chemicals, and a small spectrometer. He refined methodologies outlined in Gross' book and preferred to search clothing by hand rather than scraping or shaking. By 1920, his work was widely recognized and others had been influenced by Locard's work as well as Gross' text. Georg Popp and August Bruning in Germany and J.C. van Ledden-Hulsebosch in Holland were becoming known for their microscopic forensic wizardry.

Paul Kirk

The death of Paul Leland Kirk (1902–1970) brought an end to the brilliant and innovative career of one of Berkeley's most unusual and productive men of science. From a position of distinction and renown in biochemistry, his interest in applying scientific knowledge and techniques to the field of criminal investigation brought him ultimately to international recognition and made him the dominant figure in the emerging discipline of criminalistics.

Dr. Kirk was associated with Berkeley from the conclusion of his graduate studies in 1927 to his death. The only exception was his involvement with the Manhattan Project during the war years. He first received recognition as a microchemist, bringing to this discipline a talent and artistry that soon made him a leader in the field. His microchemistry found practical application in two areas: Tissue culture studies and criminalistics. In both these areas, a common theme is evident. At the time he became interested in them, both were more art than science. Indeed, it is doubtful that he could have involved himself in any endeavor that did not require the careful and intricate manipulation of the artist. It is to his credit that he not only elevated the art, but through his creative innovation, he helped put both areas on a sounder scientific footing.

If he wished to be remembered for any one thing, it would be for his contribution to criminalistics. Indeed, the very term "criminalistics" has come into usage largely through his efforts, and it was he who established the first academic program in criminalistics in the United States. He brought to the profession an insight and scientific rigor rarely seen before his time.

During the last two decades of his life, criminalistics occupied the major proportion of his time and energy. He was the prime mover in establishing and preserving the educational program at Berkeley, and he advised other institutions about establishing their own programs. In addition to his educational duties, he was active in professional consultation, serving both prosecution and defense. He was also increasingly concerned with problems of the profession. In particular, he desired to see criminalistics recognized, not just as a profession, but as a unique scientific discipline; this theme was the keynote of many of his publications.

Ralph Turner

Turner was born on October 18, 1917 in Milwaukee, Wisconsin. He received a B.S. degree in chemistry from the University of Wisconsin in 1939 and an M.S. in Police Administration from the University of Southern California. Turner also received additional education from Boston University Medical School and the Yale Center for Alcohol Studies.

Turner left Kansas City to go to Michigan State University (MSU). In 1949 he became involved in a year-long scientific study of drinking "under field conditions" which involved creating a social setting for four to six volunteers to gather every Friday evening to play cards, talk and drink at their leisure. The participants then agreed to have their consumption tracked and periodically submitted to alcohol-blood level testing. The National Traffic Safety Council funded this project and Turner's work paved the way for the establishment of the substance abuse program at MSU in 1976.

From 1959 through 1961, Turner served as Chief Police Advisor to the Police and Security Services of South Vietnam under the auspices of the MSU Advisory Group. He subsequently served as a Fullbright lecturer at the Central Police College of Taipei, Taiwan in 1963–1964. Appointed by the National Science Council of the Republic of China, Turner returned to the Central Police College to serve as the National Visiting Professor for 1969–1970. In addition, Turner taught short courses around the world, from Guam to Saudi Arabia. Furthermore, he developed and conducted MSU courses in comparative justice in London, England, from 1970 to 1983.

Outside of the classroom, Turner was an advisor to President Lyndon Johnson's Commission on Law Enforcement and Criminal Justice during 1965–1966 (Drunkenness Taskforce Report). In 1975 he was one of seven civilian criminology experts selected to assess the firearms evidence for the Los Angeles County Court in the assassination of Robert F. Kennedy. In fact, Turner was an expert witness throughout his career, often testifying in criminal and civil court cases related to firearms, crime scene evidence, and alcohol use. In his police consultant service, Turner worked on over 500 cases rendered in the area of criminalistics, police science and alcohol problems.

Turner was a member of numerous professional organizations and honor societies. He was a founding member of the American Academy of Forensic Science. He was recognized for his work in 1978 by the Academy of Criminal Justice Sciences in the presentation of the Bruce Smith Award, becoming the third person to receive this infrequently given honor. In 1981, he received the MSU Distinguished Faculty Award.

CHAPTER **2**

The Nature of Evidence

Evidence is central to an investigation and subsequent trial. It lays the foundation for the arguments the attorneys plan to offer. It is viewed as the impartial, objective, and sometimes stubborn information that helps a judge or jury make their conclusions. In an investigation, evidence can provide leads, clear suspects, or provide sufficient cause for arrestor indictment. In a trial, the jury or judge hears the facts or statements of the case to decide the issues. During the trial, the trier of fact (the judge or the jury, depending) must decide whether the statements made by witnesses are true or not.

Evidence can be defined as information, whether oral testimony, documents, or material objects, in a legal investigation, that makes a fact or proposition more or less likely. For example, someone is seen leaving the scene of a homicide with a baseball bat and it is later shown by scientific examination that blood removed from the bat came from the victim. This could be considered evidence that the accused person killed the victim. Having the association of the blood to the bat makes the proposition that the accused is the murderer more probable than it would be if the evidence did not exist. As will be evident later, context is crucial to a correct interpretation. If the blood was found on a shirt instead of a baseball bat, in the absence of other information, the interpretation would not change. If investigators were told, however, that the accused shirt owner had performed first aid on the bloodied victim, the significance of the evidence would need to be reconsidered.

Kinds of Evidence

Most evidence is generated during the commission of a crime and recovered at the scene, or at a place where the suspect or victim had been before or after the crime. Circumstantial evidence is evidence based on inference and not on personal knowledge or observation. Most evidence (blood, hairs, bullets, fibers, fingerprints, etc.) is circumstantial. People may think that circumstantial evidence is weak—think of TV dramas where the attorney says, "We only have a circumstantial case." But unless someone directly witnesses a crime, it is a circumstantial case and, given enough of the right kind of evidence, it could be a strong one.[1] As an example, finding fingerprints *and* fibers *and* a bag with money that has matching serial numbers to money stolen from a bank in a suspect's possession would corroborate each other. If the evidence, on the other hand, pointed to someone other than the suspect and therefore indicated his or her innocence, that would be exculpatory evidence.

Not all evidence is created equal—some items of evidence have more importance than others, as in the examples with the baseball bat and the shirt. The context of the crime and the type, amount, and quality of the evidence will determine what can be said about it. Most of the items in our daily lives including biological materials (humans have millions of hairs on their bodies, for example) are mass produced. This puts boundaries on what can be said about the people, places, and things involved in a crime.

Forensic Science Is History

Forensic science is a historical science: The events in question have already occurred and are in the past. Forensic scientists do not view the crime as it occurs; they analyze the physical remains of the criminal actions. Sciences, such as geology, astronomy, archaeology, and paleontology work in the same way—no data are seen *as they are created* but only the *remains* of events are left behind, from which data are created. Volcanoes in the Paleolithic Age, supernovae, ancient civilizations, and mastodons no longer exist but are studied now. Scientists who study ancient climates (paleoclimatologists) call the remains of these past events *proxy data* (like when someone is given the authority to represent someone else, they are called a proxy) because they represent the original data. Many sciences routinely analyze proxy data, although they may not call it that. Similarly, forensic scientists analyze evidence of past criminal events to interpret the actions of the perpetrator(s) and victim(s). Just as archaeologists must sift through layers of soil and debris to find the few items of interest at an archaeological site, forensic scientists must sort through all of the items at a crime scene (think of all the things in a typical house, for example) to find the few items of evidence that will help reconstruct

Table 2.1 Forensic science is a historical science but differs from its sibling fields in several ways

	Forensic Science	Archaeology	Geology
Time frame	Hours, days, months	Hundreds to thousands of years	Millions of years
Activity level	Personal; Individual	Social; Populations	Global
Proxy data	Mass-produced	Hand-made	Natural

the crime (table 2.1; figure 2.1). The nature and circumstances of the crime will guide the crime scene investigators and the forensic scientists to choose the most relevant evidence and examinations.

The Basis of Evidence: Transfer and Persistence

When two things come into contact, information is exchanged. Edmund Locard, a French forensic pioneer in the early part of the twentieth century, developed this principle through his study of microscopical evidence. He realized that these exchanges of information occur even if the evidence is too small to be found or identified. The results of such a transfer are proxy data: Not the transfer itself, but the "leftovers" of that contact. Forensic science reveals associations between people, places, and things through the analysis of proxy data. As previously discussed, essentially *all evidence is transfer evidence.*

The conditions that effect transfer amounts include the following:

- the pressure of the contact
- the number of contacts
- how easily the item transfers material (mud transfers more readily than does soil)
- the form of the evidence (solid, liquid, or gas)
- the amount involved in the contact

Evidence that is transferred from a source to a location with no intermediaries is said have undergone direct transfer; it has transferred from A to B. Indirect transfer involves one or more intermediate objects—the evidence transfers from A to C to B. Indirect transfer can become complicated and can pose potential limits on interpretation. For example,

(a)

(b)

Figure 2.1 (a) The exterior of a house where a crime occurred. (b) The interior, however, presents chose challenge for crime scene investigators. Courtesy Minnesota Bureau of Criminal Apprehension Forensic Laboratory

Carl owns a cat and before he goes to work each day, he pets and scratches her. At work, Carl sits in his desk chair and talks on the phone. Carl gets up to get a cup of coffee. On his return, a colleague is sitting in Carl's desk chair waiting to talk to him. Carl has experienced a direct transfer of his cat's hairs from the cat to his pants. Carl's chair, however, has received an indirect transfer of his cat's hairs—Carl's cat has never sat in his office desk chair. The colleague who sat in Carl's chair has also experienced an indirect transfer of anything on the chair, except for any fibers originating from the chair's upholstery. How to interpret finding Carl's cat's hairs on his colleague if it was not known she had sat in Carl's chair? As can be seen, while direct transfer may be straightforward to interpret, indirect transfers can be complicated and potentially misleading. It may be more accurate to speak of direct and indirect *sources*, referring to whether the originating source of the evidence is the transferring item but the "transfer" terminology has stuck.

The second part of the transfer process is persistence. Once the evidence transfers, it will remain, or persist, in that location until it further transfers (and, potentially, is lost), degrades until it is unusable or unrecognizable, or is collected as evidence. How long evidence persists depends on the following:

- what the evidence is (such as hairs, blood, toolmarks, gasoline)
- the location of the evidence
- the environment around the evidence
- time from transfer to collection
- "activity" of or around the evidence location (a living person vs. a dead body)

For example, studies demonstrate that about four hours from the time fibers are transferred 80% of them are lost through normal activity. Transfer and persistence studies with other evidence types have shown similar loss rates. This is one of the reasons why time is of the essence in processing crime scenes, identifying victims, and apprehending suspects.

Identity, Class, and Individualization

All things are unique in space and time. No two (or more) objects are absolutely identical. Take, for example, a mass-produced product such as a tennis shoe. Thousands of shoes of a particular type may be produced in a single year. The manufacturer's goal, to help sell more shoes, is to make them all look and perform the same—consumers demand consistency. This is both a help and a hindrance to forensic scientists because it makes it easy to separate one item from another (this red tennis shoe is different from that white one) but these same characteristics make it difficult to separate items with many of the same characteristics (two red tennis shoes). Think about two white tennis shoes that come off the production line one after another—how to tell them apart? A person standing on the production line might say, "this one" and "that one" but if they were mixed up, they probably could not be sorted again. They would have to be labeled somehow, as for instance numbering them "1" and "2." Even two grains of salt are different in one dimension or in their surface texture. And if they somehow were exactly the same in all respects, there would still be two of them and it is back to numbering. Now consider if the two shoes are the same except for color: One is white and one is red. They could be sorted by color but that is within the same category, "tennis shoes." But should they be put in the same category? Compared with a brown dress shoe, the two tennis shoes are more alike than they are with the dress shoes. All the shoes, however, are more alike than any of them are compared to, say, a wine cork puller. Forensic scientists have developed terminology to clarify the way they communicate about these issues.

Identification is the examination of the chemical and physical properties of an object and using them to categorize the object as a member of a group. What is the object made of? What is its color, mass, and/or volume? The following are examples of identification:

- Examining a white powder, performing one or two analyses, and concluding it is cocaine is identification
- Determining that a small colored chip is automotive paint is identification
- Looking at debris from a crime scene and deciding it contains hairs from a black Labrador retriever is identification (of those hairs)

All the characteristics used to identify an object help to refine that object's identity and its membership in various groups. The debris from the crime scene has fibrous objects in it and that restricts what they could be—most likely hairs or fibers rather than bullets— to use a ridiculous example. The microscopic characteristics would indicate that some of the fibrous objects are hairs, that they are from a dog, and the hairs are most like those from a specific breed of dog. This description places the hairs into a group of objects with similar characteristics, called a *class*. All black Labrador retriever hairs would fall into a class; these belong to a larger class of items called *dog hairs*. Further, all dog hairs can be included in the class of *nonhuman hairs* and, ultimately, into a more inclusive class called *hairs*. Going in the other direction, as the process of identification of evidence becomes more specific, it permits the analyst to classify the evidence into successively smaller classes of objects.

Class is a scalable definition—it may not be necessary to classify the evidence beyond *dog hairs* because human hairs or textile fibers are being sought. The same items can be classified differently, depending on what questions are being asked. For example, a grape, a cantaloupe, a bowling ball, a bowling pin, and a banana could be classified by *fruit v. nonfruit*, *round things versus nonround things*, and *organic versus inorganic*. Notice that the bowling pin does not fit into either of the classes in the last example because it is made of wood (which is organic) but is painted (which has inorganic components).

Stating that two objects share a class identity may indicate they come from a common source. What is meant by a "common source" depends on the material in question, the mode of production, and the specificity of the examinations used to classify the object. A couple of examples should demonstrate the potential complexity of what constitutes a common source. Going back to the two white tennis shoes, what is their common source—the factory, the owner, or where they are found? Because shoes come in pairs, finding one at a crime scene and another in the suspect's apartment could be considered useful to the investigation. The forensic examinations would look for characteristics to determine whether the two shoes were owned by the same person (the "common source"). If the question centered on identifying the production source of the shoes—based on shoeprints left at the scene—the factory would be the "common source."

Another example is fibers found on a body found in a field that are determined to be from an automobile. A suspect is arrested and fibers from his car are found to be analytically indistinguishable from the crime scene fibers. Is the suspect's car the "common source"? For investigative and legal purposes, the car should be considered so. But other models from that car manufacturer or even other car manufacturers may have used that carpeting, and the carpeting may not be the only product with those fibers. But, given the circumstances, it may be reasonable to conclude that the most logical source for the fibers is the suspect's car. If the fibers were found on the body but no suspect was developed, part of the investigation may be to determine what company made the fibers and track the products those fibers that went into in an effort to find someone who owns that product. In that instance, the "common source" could be the fiber manufacturer, the carpet manufacturer, or the potential suspect's car, depending on the question being asked.

Individualization of Evidence

To individualize evidence means to be able to put it into a class with one member. If a forensic scientist can discover properties (normally physical) of two pieces of evidence that are unique, that is, they are not possessed by any other members of the class of similar materials, then the evidence is said to have been individualized. An example would be a broken ceramic lamp: If the broken pieces of the lamp found at the crime scene can be fit with the a piece of ceramic in the burglar's tool kit, for example, then it is reasonable to conclude that those pieces of ceramic were previously one continuous piece. This conclusion implies that there is no other piece of lamp in the entire world that those broken pieces could have come from. Obviously, no one has tested these pieces of lamp against all the other, similar broken lamps to see whether they could fit. It would not be reasonable to predict or assume that two breakings would yield exactly the same number and shape of broken pieces. The innumerable variables, such as force of the blow, the thickness of the lamp, microstructure of the ceramic, chemical nature of the material, and direction of the blow, cannot be exactly duplicated and, therefore, the number and shapes of the fragments produced are, arguably, random. The probability of two (or more) breaks exactly duplicating the number and shape of fragments is unknown but generally considered to be zero. In another sense, the shapes of the fragments are not random—broken ceramics does not look like broken wood, glass, or plastic. It is easy to identify a shard of broken ceramic and recognize that it is not a splinter of wood.

Classes are defined by the number and kind of characteristics used to describe them. As an example, think of the vehicle referred to in the fictitious hit-and-run case. Up to this point, it has been referred to as a car but what if it was a pickup truck—how would that change things? Even within pickup trucks, differences can easily be drawn based only on manufacturing locations and days. Following this scheme, the number of trucks could be narrowed down to a very few sold at a particular dealership on a particular day. Classes can be scaled and are context-dependent.

Relationships and Context

The relationships between the people, places, and things involved in crimes are central to deciding what to examine and how to interpret the results. For example, if a sexual assault occurs and the perpetrator and victim are strangers, more evidence may be relevant than if they lived together or were sexual partners. Strangers are not expected to have ever met previously and, therefore, would have not transferred material before the crime. People who live together would have opportunities to transfer evidence (e.g., head hairs, pet hairs, and carpet fibers from the living room) but not others (semen or vaginal secretions). Spouses or sexual partners, being the most intimate relationship of the three examples, would share a good deal more information with the victim.

Stranger-on-stranger crimes beg the question of coincidental associations, that is, two things which previously have never been in contact with each other have items on them which are analytically indistinguishable at a certain class level. Attorneys in cross-examination may ask, "Yes, but could not [insert evidence type here] really have come from *anywhere*? Are not [generic class evidence] very *common*?" It has been proven for a wide variety of evidence that coincidental matches are extremely rare.[2–6] The variety of mass-produced goods, consumer choices, economic factors, and other product traits create a nearly infinite combinations of comparable characteristics for the items involved in any one situation.[7] Some kinds of evidence, however, are either quite common, such as white cotton fibers, or have few distinguishing characteristics, such as indigo-dyed cotton from denim fabric. In a hit-and-run case, however, finding blue denim fibers in the grill of the car involved may be significant if the victim was wearing blue jeans (or khakis!).

It is important to establish the context of the crime and those involved early in the investigation. This sets the stage for what evidence is significant, what methods may be most effective for collection or analysis, and what may be safely ignored. Using context for direction prevents the indiscriminate collection of items that clog the workflow of the forensic science laboratory. Every item collected must be transferred to the laboratory and cataloged—at a minimum—and this takes people and time. Evidence collection based on intelligent decision making, instead of fear of missing something, produces a better result in the laboratory and the courts.

Comparison of Evidence

There are two processes in the analysis of evidence. The first has already been discussed: Identification. Recall that identification is the process of discovering physical and chemical characteristics of evidence with an eye toward putting it into progressively smaller classes. The second process is comparison. Comparison is performed in order to attempt to discover the source of evidence and its degree of relatedness to the questioned material. An example may clarify this.

A motorist strikes a pedestrian with his car and then flees the scene in the vehicle. When the pedestrian's clothing is examined, small flakes and smears of paint are found embedded in the fabric. When the automobile is impounded and examined, fibers are found embedded in an area that clearly has been damaged recently. How is this evidence classified? The paint on the victim's coat is questioned evidence because the original source of the paint is not known. Similarly, the fibers found on the damaged area of the car are also questioned items. The colocation of the fibers and damaged area and the wounds/damage and paint smears are indicative of recent contact. When the paint on the clothing is analyzed, it will be compared to paint from the car; this is a known sample because it is known where the sample originated. When the fibers from the car are analyzed, representative fibers from the clothing will be collected for comparisons, which makes them known items as well. Thus, the coat *and* the car are sources of *both* kinds of items, which allows for their reassociation, but it is their *context* that makes them questioned or known. Back at the scene where the body is found there are some pieces of yellow, hard, irregularly shaped material. In the lab, the forensic scientist will examine this debris and will determine that it is plastic, rather than glass, and further it is polypropylene. This material has now been put in the class of substances that are yellow and made of polypropylene plastic. Further testing may reveal the density, refractive index, hardness, and exact chemical composition of the plastic. This process puts the material into successively smaller classes. It is not just yellow polypropylene plastic but has a certain shape, refractive index, density, hardness, and so on. In many cases this may be all that is possible with such evidence. The exact source of the evidence has not been determined, but only that it could have come from any of a number of places where this material is used—class evidence.

In a comparison, the questioned evidence is compared with objects whose source is known. The goal is to determine whether or not sufficient common physical and/or chemical characteristics between the samples are present. If they do, it can be concluded that an association exists between the questioned and known items. The strength of this association depends upon a number of factors, including the following:

- kind of evidence
- intra- and intersample variation

- amount of evidence
- location of evidence
- transfer and cross-transfer
- number of different kinds of evidence associated to one or more sources

Individualization occurs when at least one unique characteristic is found to exist in both the known and the questioned samples. Individualization cannot be accomplished by identification alone.

Finding similarities is not enough, however. It is very important that no significant differences exist between the questioned and known items. This bears on the central idea of going from "general to specific" in comparison—a significant difference should stop the comparison process in its tracks. What is a significant difference? The easiest example would be a class characteristic that is *not* shared between the questioned and known items, such as tread design on shoes or shade differences in fiber color. Sometimes the differences can be small, such as a few millimeters difference in fiber diameter, or distinct, like the cross-sectional shape of fibers or hair color.

The Method of Science

Interestingly, an important person in the history of science was not a scientist at all, but a lawyer. Sir Francis Bacon, who rose to be Lord Chancellor of England during the reign of James I, wrote a famous, and his greatest, book called *Novum Organum*. In it, Bacon put forth the first theory of the scientific method. The scientist should be a disinterested observer of the world with a clear mind, unbiased by preconceptions that might influence the scientist's understanding. This misunderstanding might cause error to infiltrate the scientific data. Given enough observations, patterns of data will emerge, allowing scientists to make both specific statements and generalizations about nature.

This sounds pretty straightforward. But it is wrong. All serious scientific thinkers and philosophers have rejected Bacon's idea that science works through the collection of unbiased observations. Everything about the way in which people work in science, from the words, the instrumentation, and the procedures, depends on our preconceived ideas and experience about how the world works. It is impossible to make observations about the world without knowing what is worth observing and what is not worth observing. People are constantly filtering their experiences and observations about the world through those things that they have already experienced. Objectivity is impossible for people to achieve.

Another important person in the philosophy of science, Sir Karl Popper, proposed that all science begins with a prejudice, a theory, a hypothesis—in short, an idea with a specific viewpoint. Popper worked from the premise that a theory can never be proved by agreement with observation, but it can be proved wrong by disagreement. The asymmetric, or one-sided, nature of science makes it unique among ways of knowing about the world: Good ideas can be proven wrong to make way for even better ideas. Popper called this aspect of science "falsifiability," the idea that a proper scientific statement must be capable of being proven false. Popper's view of constant testing to disprove statements biased by the preconceived notions of scientists replaced Bacon's view of the disinterested observer.

But Popper's ideas do not accurately describe science, either. While it may be impossible to prove a theory true, it is almost just as difficult to prove one false by Popper's methods. The trouble lies in distilling a falsifiable statement from a theory. To do so, additional assumptions that are not covered by the idea or theory itself must always be made. If the statement is shown to be false, it is not known whether it was one of the other assumptions or the theory itself that is at fault. This confuses the issue and clouds what the scientist thinks she has discovered.

Defining science is difficult. It takes a great deal of hard work to develop a new theory that agrees with the entirety of what is known in any area of science. Popper's idea about falsifiability, that scientists attack a theory at its weakest point, is simply not the way people explore the world. To show that a theory is wrong, it would take too much time, too many resources, and too many people to develop a new theory in any modern science by trying to prove every single assumption inherent in the theory false. It would be impossible!

Thomas Kuhn, a physicist by education and training who later became a historian and philosopher of science, offered a new way of thinking about science. Kuhn wrote that science involves paradigms, which are a consensual understanding of how the world works. Within a given paradigm, scientists add information, ideas, and methods that steadily accumulate and reinforce their understanding of the world. This Kuhn calls "normal science."

With time, contradictions and observations that are difficult to explain are encountered that cannot be dealt with under the current paradigm. These difficulties are set aside to be dealt with later, so as not to endanger the status quo of the paradigm. Eventually, enough of these difficulties accumulate and the paradigm can no longer be supported. When this happens, Kuhn maintains, a scientific revolution ensues that dismantles the "old" paradigm and replaces it with a new paradigm.

Kuhn's main point is that while main points of theories are tested—and some are falsified—the daily business of science is not to overturn its core ideas regularly. Falsifiability is not the only criterion for what science is. If a theory makes novel and unexpected predictions, and those predictions are verified by experiments that reveal new and useful or interesting phenomena, the chances that the theory is correct are greatly enhanced. However, science does undergo startling changes of perspective that lead to new and, invariably, better ways of understanding the world. Thus, science does not proceed smoothly and incrementally, but it is one of the few areas of human endeavor that is truly progressive. The scientific debate is very different from what happens in a court of law, but just as in the law, it is crucial that every idea receive the most vigorous possible advocacy, just in case it might be right.

In the language of science, the particular questions to be tested are called hypotheses. Suppose hairs are found on the bed where a victim has been sexually assaulted. Are the hairs those of the victim, the suspect, or someone else? The hypothesis could be framed as: "There is a significant difference between the questioned hairs and the known hairs from the suspect." Notice that the hypothesis is formed as a neutral statement that can be either proven or disproved.

After the hypothesis has been formed, the forensic scientist seeks to collect data that sheds light on the hypothesis. Known hairs from the suspect are compared with those from the scene and the victim. All relevant data will be collected without regard to whether it favors the hypothesis. Once collected, the data will be carefully examined to determine the value it has in proving or disproving the hypothesis; this is its probative value. If the questioned hairs are analytically indistinguishable from the known hairs, the hypothesis is rejected. The scientist could then conclude that the questioned hairs could have come from the suspect.

But suppose that *most* of the data suggest that the suspect is the one who left the hairs there but there are not enough data to associate the hairs to him. It cannot be said that the hypothesis has been *disproved* (there are some similarities) but neither can it be said that it has been *proved* (some differences exist but are they significant?). Although it would be beneficial to prove unequivocally that someone is or is not the source of evidence, it is not always possible. As has previously been stated, not all evidence can be individualized. The important thing to note here is that evidence analysis proceeds by forming many hypotheses and perhaps rejecting some as the investigation progresses.

Some preliminary questions must be answered before hypotheses are formulated. Is there sufficient material to analyze? If the amount of the evidence is limited, choices have to be made about which tests to perform and in what order. The general rule is to perform nondestructive tests first because they conserve material. Most jurisdictions also have evidentiary rules that require that some evidence be kept for additional analyses by opposing experts; if the entire sample is consumed in an analysis, both sides must be informed that not enough evidence will be available to perform additional analyses.

If extremely large amounts of material are submitted as evidence, how are they sampled? This often happens in drug cases where, for example, a 50 lb. block of marihuana or several kilograms of cocaine are received in one package. The laboratory must have a protocol for sampling large quantities of material so that samples taken are representative of the whole. The other kind of cases where this occurs is where there are many exhibits that appear to contain the same thing, 100 half-ounce packets of white powder. The laboratory and the scientist must decide how many samples to take and what tests to perform. This is especially important because the results of the analyses will ascribe the characteristics of the samples to the whole exhibit, such as identifying a thousand packets of powder as 23% cocaine based upon analysis of a fraction of the packets.

What happens in cases where more than one kind of analysis must be done on the same item of evidence? Consider a handgun received into evidence from a shooting incident with red stains and perhaps fingerprints on it. This means that firearms testing, serology, latent print, and possibly DNA analysis must be performed on the handgun. They should be put into an order where one exam does not spoil or preclude the subsequent exam(s). In this case, the order should be first serology, then latent print, and finally firearms testing.

It is important to note that one seemingly small piece of evidence can be subjected to many examinations. Take the example of a threatening letter one that supposedly contains anthrax or some other contagion. The envelope and the letter could be subjected to the following exams, in the following order:

- *Disease diagnosis*, to determine if it really contains the suspected contagion
- *Trace evidence*, for hairs or fibers in the envelope or stuck to the adhesives (stamp, closure, tape used to seal it)

- *DNA*, from saliva on the stamp or the envelope closure
- *Questioned documents*, for the paper, lettering, and other aspects of the form of the letter
- *Ink analysis*, to determine what was used to write the message, address, etc.
- *Handwriting*, typewriter, or printer analysis, as appropriate
- *Latent fingerprints*
- *Content analysis*, to evaluate the nature of the writer's intent and other investigative clues

In this example, the ordering of the exams is crucial not only to insure the integrity of the evidence, but also the safety of the scientists and their coworkers. Other evidence can also be very, very large—the World Trade Center towers, for example. It is important to realize that *anything* can become evidence and forensic scientists must keep open minds if they are to solve the most difficult of crimes.

CHAPTER 3

Pathology

A pathologist is a medical doctor who studies and diagnoses disease in humans. A forensic pathologist is a pathologist who has studied not only disease but trauma (wounds and damage) that leads to the death of an individual. The word "autopsy" is derived from the Greek *autopsia*, meaning seeing with one's own eyes.[1] The modern autopsy involves the standardized dissection of a corpse to determine the cause and manner of death. Regrettably, the number of autopsies has steadily declined in the past 50 years—less than 5% of hospital deaths are routinely autopsied, compared to 50% in the years after World War II.[2] This is a shame as autopsies are a quality control tool for doctors; they provide a "reality check" on their diagnoses and give them feedback on the effectiveness of treatments. Autopsies done to help solve a murder, however, are different in many ways, such as who conducts them, when and how they are conducted, and what purpose they serve to society.

Physicians have been performing autopsies for thousands of years. Greek physicians, including the famous Galen who lived during the AD second century, performed autopsies as early as the fifth century BC on criminals, war dead, and animals. Christian Europe discouraged and even forbade autopsies until the sudden death of Pope Alexander V in 1490, when it was questioned whether his successor had poisoned him. An examination found no evidence of poisoning, however. During the reign of Pope Sixtus IV (1471–1484), the plague raged through Europe causing millions of deaths. The Pope allowed for medical students at the universities in Bologna and Padua to perform autopsies in the hope of finding a cause and cure for the savage disease.

In 1530, the Emperor Charles V issued the *Constitutio Criminalis Carolina* which promoted the use of medical pathology by requiring medical testimony in death investigations. Complete autopsies were not performed, however, but this did signal an advance by mandating some medical expertise to perform the inquest.

In the 1790s, the first English pathology texts were published: Baillie's *Morbid Anatomy* (1793) and Hunter's *A Treatise on the Blood, Inflammation, and Gun-Shot Wounds* (1794). The next great advance came from the legendary Rudolf Virchow (1821–1902) who added microscopic examinations of diseased body tissues to the gross visual exam in his 1858 *Cellular Pathology*. Virchow's work signals the beginning of the modern autopsy process.

The first Medical Examiner's office in the United States was instituted in Baltimore in 1890. New York City abolished the coroner system in 1915 and established the Medical Examiner's office headed by Milton Helpern, who added toxicological exams with the help of Alexander Gettler. In 1939, Maryland established the first statewide Medical Examiner system in the United States and, in doing so, set the position of Medical Examiner apart from the political system in the state.[2-4]

Cause and Manner of Death

The cause of death is divided into the primary and secondary causes of death. The primary or immediate cause of death is a three-link causal chain that explains the cessation of life starting with the most recent condition and going backward in time. For example,

- Most recent condition (e.g., coronary bypass surgery)
  Due to, or as a consequence of:
- Next oldest condition (e.g., a rupture of the heart's lining due to tissue death from lack of oxygen)
  Due to, or as a consequence of:
- Oldest (original, initiating) condition (e.g., coronary artery disease)

Each condition can cause the one before it. At least one cause must be listed but it is not necessary to always use all three. The secondary cause of death, which includes conditions which are not related to the primary cause of death but contribute substantially to the individual's demise, such as extreme heat or frigid temperatures is typically listed.

A distinct difference exists between the standard hospital autopsy and a medicolegal autopsy. The hospital autopsy is conducted based upon a doctor's request and the family's permission—if the family denies the request for personal or religious reasons, the autopsy is not performed.

A medicolegal autopsy, however, is performed pursuant to a medical investigation of death for legal purposes.

If a person dies unexpectedly, unnaturally, or under suspicious circumstances, the coroner or medical examiner has the authority to order an examination of the body to determine the cause of death. The manner of death is the *way* in which the causes of death came to be. Generally, only four manners of death are acknowledged: Homicide, suicide, accidental, and natural. The deceased may have met their end in a way that appears suspicious to the authorities and therefore the cause and manner of death must be established. Other purposes for a medicolegal autopsy may be to identify the deceased, establish a time of death, or collect evidence surrounding the death. The cause of death is often known but the manner and mechanism of death may not be immediately obvious and are crucial to the goals of a medicolegal autopsy.

While a pathologist can perform a hospital autopsy, it takes more than normal medical training to interpret morbid anatomy and fatal trauma. In one study by Collins and Lantz (1994), trauma surgeons misinterpreted both the number and the sites of the entrance and exit wounds in up to half of fatal gunshot wounds.[5]

Coroners and Medical Examiners

The position of coroner dates from September 1194 and was initiated about 800 years ago. During the last decade of Henry II's reign, discontent had developed over the corruption and greed of the sheriffs, the law officers who represented the Crown in each English county. Sheriffs were known to extort and embezzle the populace and manipulate the legal system to their personal financial advantage—they diverted funds that should have gone to the King. A new network of law officers who would be independent of the Sheriffs was established to thwart their greedy ways and return the flow of money to the King. At that time they were "reif of the shire." Later they became known as the "Shire's reif," and then "sheriff."

The edict that formally established the Coroners was Article 20 of the "Articles of Eyre" in September, 1194. The King's Judges traveled around the countryside, holding court and dispensing justice wherever they went; this was called the "General Eyre." The Eyre of September 1194 was held in the County of Kent, and Article 20 stated:

> In Every County Of The King's Realm Shall Be Elected Three Knights And One Clerk, To Keep The Pleas Of The Crown.

And that is the only legal basis for the coroner. Coroners had to be knights and men of substance—their appointment depended on them owning property and having a sizeable income. Coroner was an unpaid position; this was intended to reduce the desire to adopt any of the Sheriffs' larcenous habits.

The most important task of the coroner was the investigation of violent or suspicious deaths; in the medieval system, it held great potential for generating royal income. All manners of death were investigated by the coroner. Interestingly, the discovering the perpetrator of a homicide was not of particular concern to the coroner—the guilty party usually confessed or ran away to avoid an almost certain hanging. The coroner was, however, concerned to record everything on his rolls, so that no witnesses, neighbors, property or chattels escaped the eagle eyes of the Justices in Eyre. There was a rigid procedure enforced at every unexpected death, any deviation from the rules being heavily fined. The rules were so complex that probably most cases showed some slip-up, with consequent financial penalty to someone. It was common practice either to ignore a dead body or even to hide it clandestinely. Some people would even drag a corpse by night to another village so that they would not be burdened with the problem. Even where no guilt lay, to be involved in a death, even a sudden natural one, caused endless trouble and usually financial loss.

The first American coroner was Thomas Baldridge of St. Mary's, Maryland Colony, appointed on January 29, 1637. He held his first death inquest two days later. It was not until 1890 that Baltimore appointed two physicians as the United State's first medical examiners.[6]

The position of coroner is by appointment or election and typically no formal education or medical training is required. Today, many coroners are funeral directors, who get possession of the body after the autopsy. This can be a major source of income to such officials.

A medical examiner, by contrast, is typically a physician who has gone through four years of university, four years of medical school, four years of basic pathology training (residency), and an additional one to two years of special training in forensic pathology. These positions are by appointment. Some states have a mixture of MEs and coroner systems while others are strictly ME or coroner systems.

The Postmortem Examination (Autopsy)

External Examination

The visual or external examination of a body starts with a description of the clothing of the deceased, photographs (including close-ups) of the body both clothed and unclothed, and a detailed examination of the entire body. Any trauma observed is noted on a form where the pathologist can make notes, sketches, or record measurements; damage to clothing should correlate to trauma in the same area on the body. Gunshot wounds are recorded, for example, to indicate entrance and exits wounds and the path of the bullet through the body. Defensive wounds that are trauma caused by victims trying to defend themselves against an attacker are also noted.

Classification of Trauma

Traumatic deaths may be classified as mechanical, thermal, chemical, or electrical. It should be noted that medical doctors and surgeons may classify wounds differently than medical examiners and forensic pathologists.

Mechanical Trauma

Mechanical trauma occurs when the force applied to a tissue, such as skin or bone, exceeds mechanical or tensile strength of that tissue. Mechanical trauma can be described as resulting from sharp or blunt force. Sharp force refers to injuries caused by sharp implements, such as knives, axes, or ice picks. It takes significantly less force for a sharpened object to cut or pierce tissue than what is required with a blunt object.

Blunt force trauma is caused by dull or nonsharpened objects, such as baseball bats, bricks, or lamps. Blunt objects produce lacerations, or tears in the tissue, typically the skin, whereas sharp objects produce incised wounds, which have more depth than length or width. The size, shape, and kind of wound may allow the forensic pathologist to determine whether a sharp or blunt object caused it. Judicious interpretations and caution are required because of the flexible nature of many of the body's tissues and the variability of the violent force. For example, a stab wound 1 in. wide, 1/8 in. thick, and 3 in. deep could have been produced by (1) a sharp object of the same dimensions, (2) a sharp object that is 1/2 in. wide, 1/8 in. thick, and 2 in. long that was thrust with great force and removed at a different angle, or (3) a sharp object larger than the stated dimensions but was only pushed in part of its length. Death from blunt and sharp trauma results from multiple processes but sharp trauma most commonly causes death from a fatal loss of blood (exsanguination) when a major artery or the heart is damaged. Blunt trauma causes death most often when the brain has been severely damaged. A contusion is an accumulation of blood in the tissues outside the normal blood vessels and is most often the result of blunt impact. The blood pressures the tissues enough to

Table 3.1 Characteristics of various gunshot wounds

GSW Class	Distance	Characteristics
Contact (entrance)	0	Blackening of the skin; lacerations from escaping muzzle gases; bright red coloration of the blood in wound from carbon monoxide gases reacting to hemoglobin in blood (carboxyhemoglobin)
Intermediate (entrance)	0.5 cm–1 m	Unburned gunpowder penetrates skin and burns it causing small red dots called *stippling*; the stippling pattern enlarges as the muzzle-to-target distance increases
Distant (entrance)	> 1 m	Speed of gunpowder is insufficient to cause stippling at this distance; lack blackening; no carboxyhemoglobin; circular defect with abraded rim; distance indeterminate
Shored exit	—	Skin is supported or *shored* by some material, such as tight clothing, wall board, or wood, as bullet exits; may look very similar to entrance GSW *except* pattern of shoring material (such as the weave of cloth) may be transferred to skin as it expands when bullet exits

break small blood vessels in the tissues and these leak blood into the surrounding area. Importantly, the pattern of the object may be transferred to the skin and visualized by the blood welling up in the tissues. An extreme contusion, a hematoma, is a blood tumor, or a contusion with more blood. The projectile from a discharged firearm produces a special kind of blunt force trauma. Table 3.1 lists the major classes of gunshot wounds (GSW), and their characteristics.

Chemical Trauma

Chemical trauma refers to damage and death which result from the interaction of chemicals with the human body.

Thermal Trauma

Extreme heat or cold also may produce death: Hypothermia is too much exposure to cold and hyperthermia is excessive heat. Both conditions not only interfere with the physiological mechanisms that keep body temperature at about 98°F/37°C, they also leave few signs at autopsy. Environmental factors—in addition to what is *not* found—may lead to a determination of hyper- or hypothermia. The sick, the very elderly, the very young, or anyone in a compromised state of health most often succumb to these conditions; factors such as alcohol, which reduces sensitivity to cold and dilates the blood vessels, speeding the cooling of the body, can aggravate the condition. Automobiles are particularly dangerous in hot climates: the inside temperature of a closed car in the sun can exceed 140°F/60°C and can be fatal to an infant in ten minutes.

Thermal burns tend to be localized and deaths from thermal injuries are due to either massive tissue damage and/or swelling of the airway causing suffocation. Persons who die in a fire do so generally because of a lack of oxygen (asphyxia) and the inhalation of combustion products, such as carbon monoxide (CO). The level of CO in the tissues can indicate whether the person was alive or dead when the fire burned them. A body from a burned building with 1 or 2% CO is presumed to have been dead (or at least not breathing) at the time the fire started.

Electrical Trauma

Electricity can cause death by a number of means. Circuits of alternating current (AC) at low voltages (<1,000 V) that cross the heart cause ventricular fibrillation, a random quivering that does not pump the blood through the body properly. The heart fibrillates because the current is acting like a (faulty) pacemaker. AC in the United States alternates from positive to negative at 3,600 times/minute and at 2,500 times/minute in Europe; the heart can only beat about 300 times/minute at maximum. A person in ventricular fibrillation for even a few minutes cannot be resuscitated. At higher voltages, the amount of current forces the heart to *stop* beating (it becomes *de*fibrillatory) causing a sustained contraction that is only broken when the circuit called tetany is broken. Although the heart can start beating normally again, such voltages immediately burn the muscle tissue.

When the clothing is removed from the deceased, care is taken to preserve any trace evidence on the clothing or the body. This will be collected and submitted to a forensic science laboratory. Wet clothes are suspended to air-dry at room temperature; special rooms or cabinets that reduce contamination are used. If wet clothes, particularly bloody one, are folded, important evidence patterns, such as blood stains, may be obscured. Equally important is the fact that folding inhibits airflow and promotes the growth of bacteria which, besides smelling bad, can damage potential DNA evidence.

The age, sex, ancestry, height, weight, state of nourishment, and any birth-related abnormalities are noted during the external exam. Death-related phenomena are also described, as these may provide information to the pathologist. For example, rigor mortis is the stiffening of the body after death. Living muscle cells transport calcium ions outside of the cells to function; calcium plays a crucial role in muscle contraction. Without this calcium transport, the muscle fibers continue to contract until they are fully contracted; the muscles release only when the tissues begin to decompose. Onset of rigor mortis begins 2–6 hours after death, starts in the smaller muscles and eventually affects even the largest ones. The stiffness remains for 2–3 days and then reduces in reverse order (largest to smallest). The rate of rigor mortis is dependent upon activity before death and the ambient temperature and the pathologist must take these into account when estimating a time since death.

After the heart no longer circulates blood through the body, it settles due to gravity. This results in a purplish discoloration in the skin, called livor mortis, also known as post mortem lividity. Because the blood is not being oxygenated in the lungs, the settled blood takes on a bluish tone. People who have died from poisons or other toxic substances, however, may not display this bluish color. For example, carbon monoxide, colors the blood a bright, cherry red and this is a good indicator of that toxic gas having been present antemortem (before death). Lividity sets in about an hour after death and reaches a peak after about three or four hours. The settled blood has coagulated and, accordingly, does not move. Therefore, the patterning of the lividity can indicate whether the body has been moved. Where pressure is applied—for example, a body lying on its back against a floor—light patches will appear where the blood could not settle. If this patterning (light patches on the back) is seen in an alleged hanging victim, the body has been tampered with.

Blood plays a role in another phenomenon that provides the forensic pathologist with information. Petechiae, pinpoint hemorrhages found around the eyes, the lining of the mouth and throat, as well as other areas, are often seen in hanging or strangulation victims. Petechiae are not conclusive evidence of strangulation or asphyxiation, however. Other phenomena, such as heart attacks or cardiopulmonary resuscitation, can induce them. In older pathology literature, they may be referred to as Tardieu spots, after the doctor who first described them. The visual examination ends with the examination of the mouth area and oral cavity (the inside of the mouth) for trauma, trace evidence, and indications of disease.

Evidence Collection at Autopsy

Other evidence is routinely collected at autopsy for submission to a forensic or toxicological laboratory. If sexual assault is suspected, three sets of swabs will be used to collect foreign body fluids. For females, a vaginal swab, an oral swab, and a rectal swab are collected; for males, oral and rectal swabs alone are taken. Each swab from one set is wiped across a separate clean glass microscope slide. These "smears" are examined microscopically for the presence of spermatozoa. The second and third sets are for other analyses, including testing for the acid phosphatase in seminal fluid and blood typing. Any other stains on the decedent's clothing or body may also be swabbed for later analysis.

Known head hairs and pubic hairs are collected during the autopsy procedure. These will be forwarded to the forensic science laboratory for comparison with any questioned hairs found on the decedent's clothing or at the crime scene. A pubic hair combing is also taken to collect any foreign materials that may be associated with the perpetrator of a sexual crime.

If the decedent's identity is unknown, a full set of fingerprints is taken to be referenced against any databases. For badly decomposed remains, the jaws may be removed to facilitate a forensic dental examination and identification.

Internal Examination and Dissection

The forensic pathologist then removes the internal organs, either all together or individually; the latter method is called the Virchow method, after the famous pathologist Rudolph Ludwig Carl Virchow (1821–1902) known for his meticulous methodology. In the Virchow method, each organ is removed, examined, weighed, and sampled separately to isolate any pathologies or evidence of disease.[7] Each organ is sectioned and viewed internally and externally. Samples for microscopic analysis of the cellular structure (histology) and for toxicology screening tests are taken. When all of the organs have been examined, they are placed in a plastic bag and returned to the body cavity.

The stomach contents, if any, are examined in detail as they can provide crucial clues to the decedent's last actions. The nature, amount, size, and condition of the contents are described, including the possibility of microscopic analysis to identify partially digested or difficult to digest materials. The small intestines may also be examined for undigested materials (corn kernels, tomato peels, among others) to determine the rate of digestion. Liquids digest faster than solids; 150 ml of orange juice empties from the stomach in about 1.5 hours, whereas the same amount of solid food may empty in 2 hours or more, depending on the density of the food. Light meals last in the stomach for 1.5–2.0 hours, medium meals up to 3 or 4 hours, and heavy meals for 4–6 hours. Food moves from the stomach in small amounts, after having been chewed, swallowed, digested, and ground into tiny pieces. A meal eaten hurriedly or gulped will last longer because it has not been properly chewed. Alcoholic beverages also delay the stomach's evacuation. Finally, a toxicological exam may be requested.

A case where stomach contents and their microscopical analysis played a role was described by forensic microscopist William Schneck of the Washington State Patrol.[8] In February of 1999, the residence of James Cochran* was found engulfed in flames and Kevin, the eleven-year-old son of James Cochran, was missing. Cochran claimed no knowledge of his son's location, suggesting Kevin had started the fire while playing with matches and had run off. Two days later, the fully clothed body of Kevin Cochran was found along a road north of Spokane. Kevin's clothing, face, and mouth exhibited a large amount of creamy brown vomit. Kevin's shoes were tied, but were on the wrong feet. At autopsy, the pathologist determined the cause of death to be strangulation. The boy's stomach contents, fingernail clipping, hand swabs, and clothing were collected as evidence for laboratory examination. That same week, James Cochran was arrested for embezzling funds from his employer.

James Cochran's pickup truck was seized and searched. Several droplets of light brown to pink material were observed on the driver's side wheel well hump, and in various locations on the mid-portion of the bed liner. The scientist collecting these droplets noted the smell of possible vomit while scrapping to recover the stains.

Stains from the bed of the pickup truck were compared to the vomit and gastric contents of Kevin Cochran. One of Kevin's sisters stated in an interview that Kevin was last seen eating cereal in the kitchen the morning

* All names have been changed.

of the fire. Investigators recovered known boxes of cereal from the Cochran's kitchen. Two opened and partially consumed plastic bags labeled *Apple Cinnamon Toastyo's*®, and *Marshmallow Mateys*®, among others, were submitted. If the cereal found in the kitchen of the Cochran residence "matched" the cereal in the vomit on Kevin's clothing, and was found to be similar to stains in the pickup truck, investigators may have a connection linking James Cochran to the death of his own son.

All the cereal brands could be distinguished microscopically. The microscopical examination and comparison of stains found on the pickup truck bed liner revealed the presence of vomit with cereal ingredients similar to those found in the vomit on Kevin's clothing and gastric fluid. The cereal ingredients were consistent with *Marshmallow Mateys*®, the final meal of Kevin Cochran. The vomit in Cochran's truck, along with other trace evidence, linked him to the death of his son, as well as the arson of his home. Investigators learned that Cochran gave a file folder containing documents, specifically the homeowners and life insurance policies of his children, to a neighbor the night after the fire.

On Memorial Day, 1999, James Cochran committed suicide in his jail cell using a coaxial cable from a television set. Investigators theorized that Cochran had killed his son and set fire to his house for the insurance money.

Determining Time since Death (Postmortem Interval)

Following death, numerous changes occur which ultimately lead to the dissolution of all soft tissues. These changes occur sequentially—although on no exact time line—and give the forensic pathologist a series of events to estimate the amount of time that has elapsed since death. The pathologist's evaluation includes changes evident upon external examination of the body, such as temperature, livor, rigor, and the extent of decomposition. Chemical changes in body fluids or tissues, in addition to any physiological changes with progression rates, such as digestion, may also give indications of the postmortem interval. Finally, any indications of survival after injuries, based upon the nature and severity of the trauma, and other factors such as blood loss. Because of the variation in these processes, the initial time range may be modified as information becomes available. Other information such as witness sightings, signed documents, or other established events may play into this initial time range.

Postmortem cooling, or algor mortis, occurs at a rate of about 2°–2.5° per hour at first and then slows to about 1.5° during the first 12 hours, and decreases further after that. The temperature is typically taken with a rectal thermometer to capture the body's inner core temperature. Many factors, such as ambient temperature, clothing, and air currents, can affect postmortem cooling and, though this method is reliable, it is known that its accuracy is low. The eyes are also an indicator of postmortem changes. Because the circulation of blood ceases, blood settles in the innermost corners of the eyes. If the eyes remain open, a thin film forms on the surface within minutes and clouds over in two to three hours; if they are closed, it may take longer for this film (an hour or more) and cloudiness (24 hours) to develop.

Decomposition of the body begins almost immediately after death and consists of two parallel processes: Autolysis, the disintegration of the body by enzymes released by dying cells, and putrefaction, the disintegration of the body by the action of bacteria and microorganisms. The body passes through four main stages of decomposition: Fresh, bloated (as the gaseous by-products of bacterial action build up in the body cavity), decay (ranging from wet to mushy to liquid), and dry. These changes depend in large part on the environmental factors surrounding the decedent, such as geographical location, seasonality, clothing, sun exposure, and animals and insects in the area.[9] Insect activity, when present, greatly assists the decomposition process.[10, 11]

Laboratory Analysis

Another routine examination requested by pathologists in medicolegal autopsies is a broad-based screen test, called a toxicology screen, or "tox screen" for short. These tests help the forensic toxicologist determine the absence or presence of drugs and their metabolites, chemicals such as ethanol and other volatile substances, carbon monoxide and other gases, metals, and other toxic chemicals in human fluids and tissues. The results help the toxicologist and the pathologist evaluate the role of any drugs or chemicals as a determinant or contributory factor in the cause and manner of death.

Autopsy Report

The autopsy report is a crucial piece of information in a death investigation. No standard method for reporting autopsy results exists, although guidelines and headings have been suggested by the College of American Pathologists.[12] Because the results of an autopsy, hospital or medicolegal, may end up in court, it is imperative that certain basic and specific information be included in every autopsy file, such as the following:

- Police report
- Medical investigator report
- Witness reports
- Medical history of the decedent

Exhumations

Humans have always had particular practices for dealing with the dead. Rituals, ceremonies, and wakes are all a part of how society acknowledges a person's passing away. One of the most common funereal practices in the United States is the embalming and burial of the dead. If questions about cause or manner of death arise once the deceased is buried, the body must be dug up or removed from the mausoleum; this process is called an exhumation. The changes wrought by death, time, and embalming practices can obliterate or obscure details that otherwise might be easily examined. Embalming is a process of chemically treating the dead human body to reduce the presence and growth of microorganisms, to retard organic decomposition, and to restore an acceptable physical appearance. Formaldehyde or formalin is the main chemicals used to preserve the body.

The forensic pathologist, when presented with challenging cases of burned, decomposed, or dismembered bodies, may consult with any of a variety of forensic specialists. Forensic anthropologists, entomologists, and odontologists, all may play a role in a death investigation. Some ME offices or forensic laboratories have one or more of these specialists on staff due to regular caseload demands. This is especially true of offices who cover a large geographical area or large metropolitan areas.

CHAPTER 4

Fingerprints

From the early days of complicated body measurements to today's sophisticated biometric devices, the identification of individuals by their bodies has been a mainstay of government and law enforcement. Computerized data bases now make it possible to compare thousands, or in the case of the FBI, *millions* of fingerprints in minutes.

The Natural-Born Criminal

Caesare Lombroso's theory of *l'umo delinquente*—the criminal man—influenced the entire history of criminal identification and criminology. Lombroso, an Italian physician in the late 1800s, espoused the idea that criminals "are evolutionary throwbacks in our midst. And these people are innately driven to act as a normal ape or savage would, but such behavior is considered criminal in our civilized society." He maintained that criminals could be identified because of the unattractive characteristics they had, their external features reflecting their internal aberrations. While normal "civilized" people may occasionally commit crimes, the natural-born criminal could not escape his mark.

Lombroso's comparison of criminals to apes made those of the lower classes and "foreigners" most similar to criminals: The "nature" of criminals was reflected in the structure of Lombroso's society. His list of criminal "traits" sounds laughable to us today: Criminals were said to have large jaws, larges faces, long arms, low and narrow foreheads, large ears, excess hair, darker skin, insensitivity to pain, and an inability to blush! It is easy to see the racial stereotypes of Lombroso's description, how society's "others" were automatically identified as criminal.

The idea of identifying "natural-born killers" caught the attention of many anthropologists and law enforcement officials in the late

1800s and, even though Lombroso's work was later repudiated (many of his assertions were not supported by objective data), it spawned a great deal of activity in the search for real, measurable traits that would assist the police in identifying criminals. One of them, a French police clerk named Alphonse Bertillon (pronounced Ber-TEE-yin), devised a complex system of anthropometric measurements, photographs, and a detailed description (what he called a *portrait parlé*) in 1883; it was later to be called Bertillonage, after its inventor. At that time, the body was considered to be constant and, as Lombroso's work then maintained, reflective of one's inner nature. Bertillon's system was devised to quantify the body; by his method, Bertillon hoped to identify criminals as they were arrested and booked for their transgressions. Repeat offenders, who today would be called career criminals or recidivists, were at that time considered a specific problem to European police agencies. The growing capitals and cities of Europe allowed for certain anonymity and criminals were free to travel from city to city, country to country, changing their names along the way as they plied their illegal trades. Bertillon hoped that his new system would allow the identification of criminals no matter where they appeared and, thus, help authorities keep track of undesirables.

Bertillonage was considered the premier method of identification for at least two decades—despite its limitations. The entire Bertillonage of a person was a complicated and involved process requiring an almost obsessive attention to detail. This made it difficult to standardize and, therefore, replicate accurately. Bertillon often lamented the lack of skill he saw in operators he himself had not trained. If the way in which the measurements were taken varied, the same person might not be identified as such by two different operators. The portrait parlé added distinctive descriptors to aid the identification process but here, again, the adjectives lacked precise objective definitions. "Lips might be 'pouting,' 'thick,' or 'thin,' 'upper or lower prominent,' with naso-labial height 'great,' or 'little' with or without a 'border,'" writes Simon Cole,[1] quoting from Bertillon's own instruction manual. What was meant by "pouting," "prominent," or "little" was better defined in Bertillon's mind than in the manual.

Bertillonage was used across Britain and in its colonies, especially India. The officials in the Bengal office were concerned with its utility, however. They wondered whether Bertillonage could distinguish individuals within the Indian population. Another concern the Bengal officials had with Bertillonage was the inconsistency between operators. There were variations in the way in which operators took the measurements, some rounded the results up and others rounded them down, and yet other operators even decided which measurements were to be taken and which ones could be ignored. Staff in the Bengal office even attempted to solve the variance problem by mechanizing the system! All these variances made searches tedious, difficult, and ultimately prone to error, defeating the point of using the method. The problem became so extreme that the Bengal office dropped Bertillonage entirely except for one small component of the system: Fingerprints.

Classification was the limiting factor in the adoption of any identification system. Bertillonage was too cumbersome and finicky to systematize for quick sorting, as were photographs. Additionally, with the growing number of individuals who were being logged into police records, any system of identification had to be capable of handling hundreds, thousands, and eventually thousands of thousands of records quickly, correctly, and remotely. It has been suggested that the limitation of searching killed Bertillonage and not its diligency or inaccuracies.[1]

Fingerprinting in the United States

The first known systematic use of fingerprint identification in the United States occurred in 1902 in New York City. The New York Civil Service Commission faced a scandal in 1900 when several job applicants were discovered to have hired better educated persons to take their civil service exams for them. The New York Civil Service Commission therefore began fingerprinting applicants to verify their identity for entrance exams and to prevent better qualified persons taking tests for unscrupulous applicants. The first set of fingerprints was taken on December 19, 1902 and was the first use of fingerprints by a government agency in the United States.[1–3]

Also in 1902, officials from the New York State Prison Department and the New York State Hospital traveled to England to study that country's fingerprint system. The following year, the New York state prison system employed fingerprints to identify criminals; the use of fingerprinting spread substantially after the United States Penitentiary in Leavenworth, Kansas established a fingerprint bureau. This established the first use of fingerprints for criminal identification in the United States. John K. Ferrier of Scotland Yard taught the techniques and methods of fingerprinting to the public and law enforcement in attendance at the 1904 World Fair in St. Louis. Because of the popularity of the Fair and the novelty of fingerprints as a "modern" forensic method, the public and professional awareness of fingerprinting blossomed in the United States.[2]

Thomas Jennings was the first U.S. criminal convicted by using fingerprint evidence. Charles Hiller had been murdered during a burglary in Chicago and Jennings was charged and tried for the crime. He was convicted in 1911. The International Association for Identification (IAI) was formed in 1915 initially as a professional association for "Bertillon clerks" but as fingerprinting grew and eventually replaced Bertillonage, the focus of the IAI also changed.* *The Finger Print Instructor* by Frederick Kuhne was published in 1916 and is considered the first authoritative textbook on fingerprinting in the United States.[1]

The growing need for a national repository and clearinghouse for fingerprint records led to an Act of Congress on July 1, 1921 that established the Identification Division of the FBI in Washington, DC in 1924. A boost to the noncriminal use of fingerprinting came in 1933 when the United States Civil Service Commission (now the Office of Personnel Management) submitted over 140,000 government employee and applicant fingerprints to the FBI's Identification Division; this prompted the FBI to establish a Civil Identification Section, whose fingerprint files would eventually expand well beyond the Criminal Files. In 1992, the Identification Division was renamed the Criminal Justice Information Services Division (CJIS) and is now housed in Clarksburg, West Virginia. Fingerprint case work submitted to the FBI is conducted at their Laboratory Division in Quantico, Virginia.

What Are Friction Ridges?

Friction ridges appear on the palms and soles of the ends of the fingers and toes. These ridges are found on the palms and soles of all primates (humans, apes, monkeys, and prosimians); in primates with prehensile tails ("fingerlike" tails, such as spider monkeys), friction ridges also appear on the volar surface of the tails. All primates have an arboreal evolutionary heritage: Trees have been and continue to be the primary habitat for most apes and monkeys and humans share this arboreal heritage. Primates' hands and feet show adaptations for locomotion and maneuvering in the branches of trees. The opposable thumb provides a flexible and sturdy means of grasping branches or the food that hangs from them. Primates, unlike other mammals such as squirrels or cats, have

---

* More information on the IAI can be found at www.theiai.org.

nails instead of claws at the distal end of their phalanges. Claws would get in the way of grasping a branch (imagine making a fist with 2-inch nails) and would provide insufficient structure to hold an animal with a high body weight (a 1 lb. squirrel is highly maneuverable in a tree but a 150 lb. jaguar is not). The ridges on the palms and soles provide friction between the grasping mechanism and whatever it grasps. Without them, it would be nearly impossible to handle objects in our environment.

Friction ridges develop in the womb and remain the same throughout life, barring some sort of scarring or trauma to the deep skin layer. This deep skin layer acts as a template for the configuration of the friction ridges seen on the surface of the skin. Although people grow and increase in size, the friction ridges on our bodies, which became permanent and fixed in their patterns from about 17 weeks of embryonic development, our friction ridge patterns do not change like other parts of our bodies.[4]

What Is a Friction Ridge Print Made Of?

A friction ridge *print* is a representation of a friction ridge *pattern* in some medium. Friction ridge prints can be classified as either patent, if they are visible with the unaided eye, or latent, if they require some sort of assistance to make them visible. Patent prints can appear because of some transferable material on the ridge pattern, such as liquid blood, liquid paint, or dust, or because the ridge pattern was transferred to a soft substrate that had "memory" and retained the impression, like clay, soft spackle, or wax. Often a patent print is doubly important: Finding the suspect's fingerprint is good but finding it imprinted in the victim's blood is extremely telling!

Latent prints are composed of the sweat and oils of the body that are transferred from the ridge pattern to some substrate. By themselves, they are not usually visible to the naked eye. The most familiar method for making prints visible is the use of fingerprint powder. Fingerprint powders are colored, fluorescent, or magnetic materials that are very finely ground and are brushed lightly over a suspected print to produce contrast between the background and the now visible print. These powders typically are available in black, white, and other colors, including metallic. Black is the most popular color because it creates the most contrast on a white card, commonly used for filing and recording friction ridge prints. This provides a uniform medium for the comparison of black ridges of the questioned print to the black inked ridges of the known print.

Principles of Friction Ridge Analysis

Since Galton's time, friction ridges have been considered unique; that is, no individual's friction ridges are identical to anyone else's. The concept of uniqueness is typically associated with the philosopher Gottfried Wihelm Leibniz who stated "For in nature there are never two beings which are perfectly alike and in which it is not possible to find an internal difference, or at least a difference founded upon an intrinsic quality." While it is one thing to understand all people and things are separate in space and time, it is quite another to prove it.

Galton was the first to attempt to calculate the likelihood of finding two friction ridge patterns that are the same. Numerous researchers have recalculated this probability over the years by various calculations based on differing assumptions. But they all indicate that the probability of any one particular fingerprint is somewhere between 0.000000954 and 1.2×10^{-80}, all very small numbers. Technically, even infinitesimal probabilities such as these are still *probabilities* and do not represent true uniqueness[5] (which would be a probability of 1 in) but the values are such that latent fingerprints, with sufficient minutiae, can be considered unique by the vast majority of forensic scientists and the courts (table 4.1).

Under low-power magnification (typically 10x), friction ridge patterns are studied for the kind, number, and location of various ridge characteristics or minutiae. As with many other types of forensic evidence, it is not merely the presence or absence of minutiae that makes a print unique: It is the *presence, kind, number,* and, especially, *arrangement* of those characteristics that are important. When two or more prints are compared, it is a careful point-by-point study to determine whether enough of the significant minutiae in the known print are present in the questioned print, with no relevant differences.

The majority of prints that are identified, resolved, and compared are partial prints, representing only a portion of the complete print pattern. A friction ridge scientist must then determine whether a partial print is suitable for comparison, that is, whether the print has the necessary *and* sufficient information to allow a proper comparison. A partial print, or even a complete print for that matter, may be identifiable as such but be smudged, too grainy, or too small for the scientist to make an accurate and unbiased comparison. Often this is the crucial step in a friction ridge print examination that is dependent on the scientist's experience, visual acuity, and judgment.[3]

Table 4.1 Comparison of probability of a particular fingerprint configuration using different published models for 36 minutiae and 12 minutiae (matches involve full not partial matches)[a]

Author	Probability Value for a Latent Print with 36 Minutiae	Probability Value for a Latent Print with 12 Minutiae
Galton (1892)	1.45×10^{-11}	9.54×10^{-7}
Henry (1900)	1.32×10^{-23}	3.72×10^{-9}
Balthazard (1911)	2.12×10^{-22}	5.96×10^{-8}
Boze (1917)	2.12×10^{-22}	5.96×10^{-8}
Wentworth and Wilder (1918)	6.87×10^{-62}	4.10×10^{-22}
Pearson (1930, 1933)	1.09×10^{-41}	8.65×10^{-17}
Roxburgh (1933)	3.75×10^{-47}	3.35×10^{-18}
Cummins and Midlo (1943)	2.22×10^{-63}	1.32×10^{-22}
Trauring (1963)	2.47×10^{-26}	2.91×10^{-9}
Gupta (1968)	1.00×10^{-38}	1.00×10^{-14}
Osterburg et al. (1977)	1.33×10^{-27}	1.10×10^{-9}
Stoney (1985)	1.20×10^{-80}	3.5×10^{-26}

[a] S. Pankanti, S. Prabhakar, and A. K. Jain. *On the Individuality of Fingerprints*, in *Computer Vision and Pattern Recognitions (CVPR)*. 2001. Hawaii.

Classifying Fingerprints

The patterning and permanency of friction ridges allows for their classification. As discussed earlier, the fact that fingerprints could be systematically sorted and cataloged was a main reason for their widespread adoption among government agencies. But it is important to keep in mind that it is the general patterns, and not the individualizing elements that makes possible this organization.

The first person to describe a taxonomy of fingerprints was Dr. Jan Purkyně, a Czech physician and one of the giants in the history of physiology. In 1823, Dr. Purkyně lectured on friction ridges in humans and primates and described a system of nine different basic ridge patterns. In 1880, Dr. Henry Faulds, a Scot who worked in a Tokyo hospital, had researched fingerprints after noticing some on ancient pottery; Faulds had even used "greasy finger-marks" to solve the theft of a bottle of liquor. He published his research on the use and classification of fingerprints in a letter to the scientific journal *Nature*. The publication of Faulds' letter drew a quick response from William Herschel, a chief administrator from the Bengal British Government Office in India, who claimed that he, not Faulds, had prior claim to the technique of fingerprints. Herschel had been using finger and palm prints to identify contractors in Bengal since the Indian Mutiny of 1857, employing a simplistic version of the system that Henry eventually instituted some 40 years later. In fact, it may not have been Herschel's own idea to use prints for identification: The Chinese and Assyrians used prints as "signatures" since at least 9,000 years before the present. The Indians had probably borrowed this behavior and Henry had adopted it though local customs. Herschel had tried to institute fingerprinting as the primary means of identification across all of India; his supervisor thought otherwise and Herschel's work languished until Fauld's letter was published. The argument between Fauld and Herschel about who was first would continue into the 1950s.

Today, all fingerprints are divided into three main classes: Loops, arches, and whorls. Loops have one or more ridges entering from one side of the print, curving back on themselves, and exiting the fingertip on the same side (figure 4.1). If the loop enters and exits on the side of the finger towards the little finger, it is called an ulnar loop, being the forearm bone on that side. If the loops enters and exits on the side towards

Figure 4.1 A loop is a fiction ridge pattern where one or more ridges enter upon either side, recurve, touch or pass an imaginary line between delta and core and pass out, or tend to pass out, on the same side the ridges entered. www.nist.gov

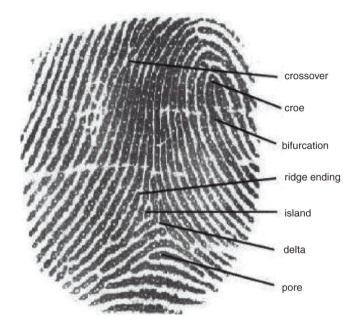

crossover

croe

bifurcation

ridge ending

island

delta

pore

Figure 4.2 The anatomy of a fingerprint

the thumb, it is termed a radial loop. All loops are surrounded by two diverging ridges; the point of divergence is called a delta because of its resemblance to a river delta and the Greek letter (*delta*). The central portion of the loop is called the core (figure 4.2).

Arches are the rarest of the three main classes of patterns. Arches are either plain, with ridges entering one side of the finger, gradually rising to a rounded peak, and exiting the other side, or tented, which are arches with a pronounced, sharp peak (figure 4.3). A pattern that resembles a loop but lacks one of the required traits to be classified as a loop can also be designated as a tented arch. Arches do not have type lines, cores, or deltas.

Whorls are subdivided into plain whorl, central pocket loop, double loop, and accidental, as depicted. All whorls have type lines and at least two deltas (figure 4.4). Central pocket loops and plain whorls have a minimum of one ridge that is continuous around the pattern but it does not necessarily have to be in the shape of a circle; it can be an oval, ellipse, or even a spiral. Plain whorls located between the two deltas of the whorl pattern and central pocket loops are not. This difference can be easily determined by drawing a line equidistant between the two deltas: If the line touches the circular core, then the whorl is a plain whorl; if not, it is a central pocket loop.

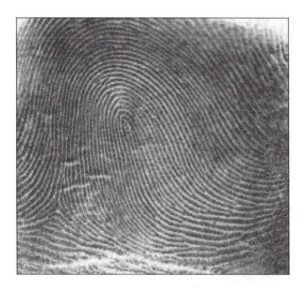

Figure 4.3 An arch is a fiction ridge pattern where the ridges enter on one side of the impression, and flow, or tend to flow, out the other with a rise or wave in the center. www.nist.gov

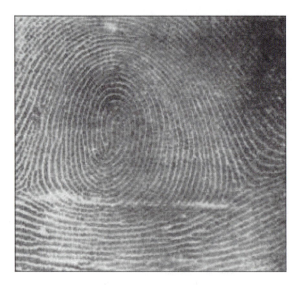

Figure 4.4 A whorl is a fiction ridge pattern where one or more ridges which make, or tend to make, a complete circuit, with two deltas, between which, when an imaginary line is drawn, at least one recurring ridge within the inner pattern area is cut or touched. www.nist.gov

Other, rarer patterns exist. A double loop is made up of two loops that swirl around each other. Finally, an accidental is a pattern that combines two or more patterns (excluding the plain arch) and/or does not clearly meet the criteria for any of the other patterns.

Classification

The modern system of fingerprint classification is based on Henry's original design, which could process a maximum of 100,000 sets of prints, with modifications by the FBI to allow for the huge number of entries that have accumulated over the years. The FBI Criminal Justice Information Section (CJIS) currently has over 80 million fingerprints stored in its files.

The modern fingerprint classification consists of a primary classification that encodes fingerprint pattern information into two numbers derived as given below. All arches and loops are considered "non-numerical" patterns and are given a value of zero. Whorls are given the values depending on which finger they appear:

Right thumb, right index	16
Right middle, right ring	8
Right little, left thumb	4
Left index, left middle	2
left ring, left little	1

The values are summed, with one added to both groups, and the resulting primary classification is displayed like a fraction:

R index + R ring + L thumb + L middle + L little + 1
R thumb + R middle + R little + L index + L ring + 1

If, for example, all of your fingers had whorls, the formula would be:

16+8+4+2+1+1/16+8+4+2+1+1 = 32/32

If all of your fingers had arches or loops instead, the formula would be:

0+0+0+0+0+1/0+0+0+0+0+1 = 1/1.

In and of itself, a primary classification is just that: Class evidence.* The primary classification was originally devised to sort individuals into

---

* Be careful: "Identification" to a finger print scientist means "unique" or one-of-a-kind; this is a different meaning than when a forensic chemist states that a white powder has been "identified" as cocaine.

smaller, more easily searched, categories; this, of course, was when fingerprints were searched by hand. Additional subdivisions of the classification scheme may be used but they still only serve as a sieve through which to organize and efficiently search through filed prints. The problem with storing and sorting fingerprints using only the Henry-FBI classification system is that, while the system stores all ten prints as a set, rarely are full sets of fingerprints found at a crime scene. To search through even a moderately sized data base of ten-print sets (called "ten prints") for an individual print would take too long and be too prone to error. Many agencies used to keep single-print files which contained the separate fingerprints of only the most frequent, locally repeating criminals, the "usual suspects."

Automated Fingerprint Identification Systems (AFIS)

The advent of computers heralded a new age for many forensic sciences and among the first to utilize the technology was the science of fingerprints. Capturing, storing, searching, and retrieving fingerprints via computer is now a standard practice among police agencies and forensic science laboratories. Automated fingerprint identification systems, or AFIS (pronounced "AYE-fis"), are computerized databases of digitized fingerprints that are searchable through software. An AFIS can store millions of prints which can be searched in a matter of minutes by a single operator. The core of this electronic system is a standard format developed by the FBI and the National Institute of Standards and Technology (NIST), with the advice of the National Crime Information Center (NCIC), which provides for the conversion of fingerprints into electronic data and their subsequent exchange via telecommunications and computers. Although the data format was a standard, the software and computers that operate AFIS are not and several vendors offer products to law enforcement and forensic science agencies. The drawback was that these products were not compatible with each other, precluding the easy exchange of information between systems.[6]

This situation began to change in 1999 when the FBI developed and implemented a new automated fingerprint system known as the Integrated Automated Fingerprint Identification System or IAFIS (pronounced "EYE-aye-fis"). Although IAFIS is primarily a ten-print system for searching an individual's fingerprints like a standard AFIS, it can also digitally capture latent print and ten-print images and then

- enhance an image to improve its quality;
- compare crime scene fingerprints against known ten-print records retrieved from the data base;
- search crime scene fingerprints against known fingerprints when no suspects have been developed; and
- automatically search the prints of an arrestee against a data base of unsolved cases.

Other advances are being made to solve the problem of noncompatible AFIS computers. The Universal Latent Workstation is the first in a new generation of interoperable fingerprint workstations. Several state and local agencies, the FBI, NIST, and AFIS manufacturers are developing standards to provide for the interoperability and sharing of fingerprint identification services. Agencies will eventually be able to search local, state, neighboring and the FBI IAFIS system, all with a single entry. Sadly, though, as of 2006, only 35 states can communicate with the FBI's fingerprint system.

How Long Do Friction Ridge Prints Last?

Plastic prints will last as long as the impressed material remains structurally intact. The life of a print left in some medium, such as blood or dust, is quite fragile and short. Latent prints, however, can, in the proper environments, last for years. Therefore, the age of a set of fingerprints is almost impossible to determine.

Elimination Prints

As with any other type of evidence, obtaining known samples for elimination purposes can be of great assistance to the forensic scientist. These may not only eliminate individuals from an investigation's focus but they can also demonstrate a proper scientific mind-set through a comprehensive series of comparisons. If these eliminated knowns are incorporated into a trial presentation, it can create confidence in the mind of the trier of fact that, not only do the defendant's known prints match, but the other potential subjects' prints do *not* match. Displaying what is and is not a match can clarify the forensic scientist's process of identification and comparison to the layperson.

CHAPTER 5

Trace Evidence

Trace evidence is a category of evidence that is characterized by materials that, because of their size or texture, are easily transferred from one location to another. When two things come into contact, information is exchanged. This is the central guiding principle of forensic science. Developed by Edmund Locard, it posits that this exchange of information occurs, even if the results are not identifiable or are too small to be found. In this sense, evidence is like pronouns in language: the thing itself is rarely examined *sui generis* but either bits of it that have transferred or something transferred to it that *represent* the thing (a noun, to extend the metaphor).[1] Once transferred, they persist for some period of time until they are collected as evidence, lost through activities, or ignored. The analysis of trace evidence reveals associations between people, places, and things involved in criminal activity.[2]

The category "trace evidence" encompasses a variety of materials, natural and manufactured, that require microscopy to identify and analyze. Additional instrumentation, which may have microscopes attached to assist in the location and analysis of these minute mute witnesses, is also employed. These materials include, but are not limited to, glass, soils, hairs, fibers, paint, pollen, wood, feathers, dust, and other detritus of things that surround us in our lives.[3, 4]

Contamination

Once the activity surrounding the crime has stopped, any transfers that take place may be considered contamination—an unwanted transfer of information between items of evidence. A wet bloody shirt from a homicide victim must not be packaged with clothes from a suspect; the postcrime transfers might obscure the criminal evidence.

Every item of evidence (where practical) should be packaged separately. Contamination is itself a kind of evidence and may prove sloppy or careless forensic work. It is impossible to prevent any contamination but properly designed facilities, adequate protective clothing, and quality-oriented protocols that specify the handling and packaging of evidence can help to minimize it.[5]

Hairs

Hairs are a fibrous structure originating from the skin of mammals. Nonmammalian animals and plants have structures that may appear to be hairs (and erroneously named thus) but they are not: Only mammals have hairs. Hairs grow from the epidermis of the body. The follicle is the structure within which hairs grow; hairs grow from the base of the follicle upwards (figure 5.1). Hair is made of keratin, a protein-based material also found in nails and horns. In the follicle, the hair is still soft; as the hair proceeds up the follicle, it dries out and hardens and this process is called keratinization.

Hairs have three growth phases. In the anagen (active) phase, the follicle produces new cells and pushes them up the hair shaft becoming incorporated into the hair. Specialized cells (melanocytes) in the follicle produce small, colored granules, called melanin or pigment, which give hairs their color. The combination, density, and distribution of these

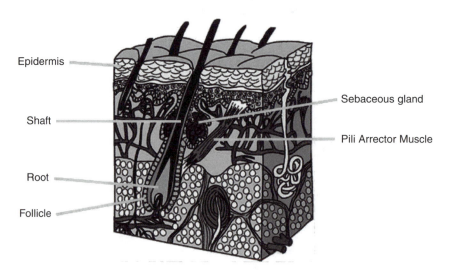

Figure 5.1 The anatomy of a hair follicle

granules produce the range of hair colors seen in humans and animals. Hairs stay in the anagen phase for a length of time proportional to their body area; scalp hairs may stay in anagen for several years, for example. Head hairs grow at an average of ½ inch (1.3 cm) per month. After the anagen phase, the hair transitions into the catagen (resting) phase. During the catagen phase, the follicle shuts down production of cells, which begin to shrink, and the root condenses into a bulb-shaped structure, called a root bulb or a club root. The transitioned hair now enters telogen phase (resting) of the follicle—cell production has ceased, the root is condensed, and is held in place mechanically. When the hair falls out, the follicle is triggered into anagen phase again and the cycle renews. On a healthy human head, about 80% to 90% of the hairs are in the anagen phase, about 2% in the catagen phase, and about 10% to 18% in the telogen phase. Humans, on average, lose about 100 scalp hairs a day.[6]

A single hair on a macroscale has a root, a shaft, and a tip (figure 5.2). The root is that portion that resided in the follicle. The shaft is the main portion of the hair and the tip is the portion furthest from the scalp. Internally, the three main structural elements in a hair are the cuticle, the cortex, and the medulla. The cuticle of a hair is a series of overlapping layers of scales that form a protective covering. Animal hairs have scale patterns that vary by species and that are a useful diagnostic tool for identifying them. Humans have a scale pattern called imbricate; this pattern does not vary significantly between people and is generally not useful in forensic examinations.

The cortex makes up the bulk of the hair and consists of spindle-shaped cells that contain or constrain other structures. Pigment granules are found in the cortex and they are dispersed variably throughout the cortex.

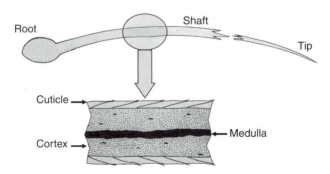

Figure 5.2 A hair consists of a root, a shaft, and a tip. Microscopically it has a medulla, cortex, and a cuticle

The granules vary in size, shape, aggregation, and distribution—all excellent characteristics for forensic comparisons.

It is easy to determine whether a hair is human or nonhuman by a microscopic examination. Determining the species of the nonhuman hair takes effort, skill, and a good reference collection. Animal hairs have macroscopic and microscopic characteristics that distinguish them from those of humans.

Unlike other animals, humans exhibit a wide variety of hairs on their bodies. The characteristics of these hairs may allow for an estimation of body area origin. The following are typical body areas that can be determined:

- head (or scalp)
- pubic
- facial
- chest
- axillary (armpits)
- eyelash/eyebrow and
- limb

Typically, only head and pubic hairs are suitable for microscopic comparison; facial hairs may also be useful. Hairs that do not fit into these categories may be called transitional hairs, such as those on the stomach. It may be difficult to make a decision as to the body area of origin; it may not matter to the circumstances of the crime. Labeling the hair as a "body hair" is sufficient and may be the most accurate conclusion, given the quality and nature of the hair. Doing so, however, precludes that hair from further microscopic examination.

Estimating the ethnicity or ancestry of an individual from his or her hairs is just that: An estimate. The morphology and color of a hair can give an indication of a person's ancestry. Humans are more variable in their hair morphology than any other primate. This variation tends to correlate with a person's ancestry although it is not exact. For simplicity and accuracy, three main ancestral groups are used: Europeans, Africans, and Asians. In the older anthropological and forensic literature, these groups were referred to as, respectively, Caucasoids, Negroids, and Mongoloids; these terms are archaic now and should not be used. Because an examiner estimates a hair to be from a person of a certain ancestry does not mean that is how that person identifies himself or herself racially.[7]

Misconceptions abound about hairs and about what can be derived from their examination. Age and sex cannot be determined from examining hairs; gray hairs may occur from a person's 20s onward and long hair does not mean "female" just as short hair does not mean "male." Hairs do not grow after you die (skin shrinks from loss of water) and, despite some studies to the contrary, shaving does not stimulate hair growth.

The goal of most forensic hair examinations is the microscopic comparison of a questioned hair or hairs to a known hair sample. A known hair sample consists of between 50 and 100 hairs from all areas of interest, typically the head or pubic area. The hairs must be combed and pulled to collect both telogen and anagen hairs. A known sample must be representative of the collection area to be suitable for comparison purposes.[6]

A comparison microscope is used for the examination. A comparison microscope is composed of two transmitted light microscopes joined by an optical bridge to produce a split image. This side-by-side, point-by-point comparison is key to the effectiveness and accuracy of a forensic hair comparison: Hairs cannot be compared properly otherwise. The hairs are examined from root to tip, at magnifications of ×40 to ×250. Hairs are mounted on glass microscope slides with a mounting medium of an appropriate refractive index for hairs, about 1.5. All the characteristics present are used; no set list exists for hair traits. The known sample is characterized and described to capture its variety. The questioned hairs are then described individually. These descriptions cover the root, the microanatomy of the shaft, and the tip. Like must be compared to like: Pubic hairs to pubic hairs and head hairs to only head hairs.

Three conclusions can be drawn from a forensic microscopic hair comparison. If the questioned hair exhibits the same microscopic characteristics as the known hairs, it could have come from the same person who provided the known sample. Hair comparisons are not a form of positive identification, however. If the questioned hair exhibits similarities but slight differences to the known hair sample, no conclusion can be drawn as to whether the questioned hair could have come from the known source. Finally, if the questioned hair exhibits different microscopic characteristics from the known hair sample, then it can be concluded that the questioned hair did not come from the known source. This evaluation and balancing of microscopic traits within and between samples is central to the comparison process.

Given other sciences, it might seem that hairs could be coded, entered into a database, and statistics applied. This would be of immense help in determining the significance of hairs as evidence. A hair's traits could be entered as a query and at the push of a button a frequency of occurrence for a population could be calculated. But it is not as easy as that.

The late Barry Gaudette, a hair examiner with the Royal Canadian Mounted Police did a study to assess the specificity of microscopic hair examinations.[8, 9] Gaudette's work involved brown head hairs of European ancestry, coded and intercompared. The study determined that only nine pairs of hairs were indistinguishable, resulting in a frequency of 1 in 4,500. He did further work with pubic hairs which resulted in a frequency of 1 in 1,600.[9] Although critics complained that the study was flawed and the frequencies are not valid for any other sample, it was the first clinical study of its kind. Some examiners quoted these frequencies in their testimony to quantify the significance of their findings—a completely unjustified and erroneous application of the study. A later paper by Gaudette's colleagues[10] elaborated on his study and refined the frequencies. Other smaller studies provided additional insights into what the potential specificity of microscopic hair examinations might be but, to date, no universal approach for calculating significance has been published. And probably none will be.[11] Hairs are a very complicated composite biological material and the expression of hair traits across the population is highly variable. Being three-dimensional makes quantifying the traits that much more difficult. While a computer could be used to analyze digital images and categorize the hairs, a human could do it much faster and just as accurately. And now that DNA analysis is more accessible, this approach is hardly justified.

The advent of forensic mitochondrial DNA (mtDNA) in the mid-1990s heralded a new era of biological analysis in law enforcement. This was especially true for hairs, as it offered a way to add information to microscopic hair examinations. The microscopic comparison of human hairs has been accepted scientifically and legally for decades. Mitochondrial DNA sequencing added another test for assessing the significance of attributing a hair to an individual. Neither the microscopic nor molecular analysis alone, or together, provides positive identification. The two methods complement each other in the information they provide. For example, mtDNA typing can often distinguish between hairs from different sources although they have similar, or insufficient, microscopic hair characteristics. Hair comparisons with a microscope, however, can often distinguish between samples from maternally related individuals where mtDNA analysis is "blind."

In a recent study,[12] the results of microscopic and mitochondrial examinations of human hairs submitted to the FBI Laboratory for analysis were reviewed. Of 170 hair examinations, there were 80 microscopic associations; importantly, only nine were excluded by mtDNA. Also, 66 hairs that were considered either unsuitable for microscopic examinations or yielded inconclusive microscopic associations were able to be analyzed with mtDNA. Only 6 of these hairs did not provide enough mtDNA and another three yielded inconclusive results. This study demonstrates the strength of combining the two techniques. It is important to realize that microscopy is not a "screening test" and mtDNA analysis is not a "confirmatory test." Both methods, or either, can provide important information to an investigation. One test is not better than the other because they both analyze different characteristics. The data in the FBI study support the usefulness of both methods—and this is echoed in the expanding use of both microscopical and mitochondrial DNA examinations of hairs in forensic cases.

Fibers

Textile fibers are "common" in the sense that textiles surround us in our homes, offices, and vehicles. We are in constant contact with a dazzling diversity of textiles. We move through a personal environment of clothing, cars, upholstery, things we touch, and people we encounter. Textile fibers are also neglected and undervalued as forensic evidence. Fibers provide many qualitative and quantitative traits for comparison. Textile fibers are often produced with specific end-use products in mind (underwear made from carpet fibers would be very uncomfortable) and these end-uses lead to a variety of discrete traits designed into the fibers. It is rare to find two fibers at random that exhibit the same microscopic characteristics and optical properties.

Applying statistical methods to trace evidence is difficult, however, because of a lack of frequency data. Very often, even the company that made a particular fiber will not know how many products those fibers went into. Attempts have been made to estimate the frequency of garments in populations; for example, based upon databases from Germany and England, the chance of finding a woman's blouse made of turquoise acetate fibers among a random population of garments was calculated to be nearly 4 in 1 million garments.

Color is another powerful discriminating characteristic. About 7,000 commercial dyes and pigments are used to color textiles and no one dye is used to create any one color and millions of shades of colors are possible in textiles.[13]

A competent and properly equipped forensic fiber examiner, using established and modern methods of analysis, will be able to identify a fiber as natural (animal, vegetable, or mineral) or manufactured; if manufactured, its generic and subgeneric class can also be identified. The analysis will also determine whether or not a questioned fiber sample is consistent with originating from a known textile source. A forensic fiber examiner must employ a comparison microscope and a compound light microscope equipped with polarized light capability; these may be the same instrument. A complete study of fibers is aided by knowledge of chemistry, physics, biology, microscopy, manufacturing, business, and the textile industry. In daily work, the forensic fiber examiner may use only a few of these skills, but a working knowledge of fiber production, marketing, microscopy, and chemical properties is desirable.[14]

Fibers can occur in virtually any type of crime and can be found in many locations. A distinction should be made between "native" and "foreign" fibers. Native fibers are those that come from one item, such as a sweater or upholstery. Textiles from that environment are possible, and expected, donors to other things in that environment. It would not be surprising to find fibers from your sweater on the couch where you have been sitting, for example. Foreign fibers are those that occur in a different environment and are transferred into an unrelated "native" environment. For example, the clothed body of a victim is found wrapped in a blanket which did not belong to the victim. The clothing is a source of fibers that may be transferred to the blanket. The clothing fibers are foreign to the blanket and the blanket fibers are foreign to the clothing. Because of their contact, fibers from the blanket, the clothing or both may be transferred. This exchange of fibers illustrates the Locard exchange principle—one of the fundamental tenets of forensic science and criminal investigation. The Locard exchange principle states that whenever two objects or persons come into contact, evidence is exchanged; this evidence may be too small to be noticed or recovered.[15]

The types of crimes in which fibers may play a role are almost limitless. However, there are a few types in which fibers are especially important. These include crimes of violent contact, including homicide and sexual assault. In the latter, fibers are frequently accompanied by hair evidence. Hit-and-run cases in which a pedestrian is involved often result in the transfer of fibers from the pedestrian's clothing to a surface on the vehicle. Transfer of fibers may also be expected whenever a vehicle is involved in transportation of the victim or perpetrator.

A classic example of the importance of fibers in a murder case is the Atlanta child murders involving Wayne Williams. In this case, much of the crucial evidence linking the defendant to 12 of 28 murders of children over a two-year period was obtained by comparison of 62 fibers obtained from the bodies and their clothing to fibers in the defendant's environment, including his body, his home, and his cars. This case also demonstrated the use of statistics in estimating the frequency of occurrence of a particular type of carpet fiber found in the William's home.[16, 17] Another example is that of the fiber evidence in the O.J. Simpson case; regrettably, the evidence, although strong, went largely unheeded.[18] Other examples of the utility of fiber evidence abound.[4, 19]

It is rare to find two fibers at random that exhibit the same microscopic characteristics and optical properties; for example, based upon data bases from Germany and England, the chance of finding a woman's blouse made of turquoise acetate fibers among a random population of garments was calculated to be nearly 4 in one million garments.

Textile Fibers

A textile fiber is a unit of matter, either natural or manufactured, that forms the basic element of fabrics and other textile structures. Specifically, a textile fiber is characterized having a length at least 100 times its diameter and a form that allows it to be spun into a yarn or made into a fabric by various methods. Fibers differ from each other in chemical structure, cross-sectional shape, surface contour, color, as well as length and width.

The diameter of textile fibers is small, generally 0.0004 to 0.002 in.[15] or 11 to 50 micrometers (μm). Their length varies from about 7/8 in. or 2.2 cm to many miles. Based on length, fibers are classified as either filament or staple fiber. Filaments are a type of fiber having indefinite or extreme length, such as synthetic fibers which can be made to any length; silk is the only naturally occurring filament. Staple fibers are natural fibers or cut lengths of filament, typically being 1.5 to 8 in. (3.75 to 28.5 cm) in length.[20]

The size of natural fibers is usually given as a diameter measurement in micrometers. The size of silk and manufactured fibers is usually given in denier (in the United States) or tex (in other countries). Denier and tex are linear measurements based on weight by unit length. The denier is the weight in grams of 9,000 meters of the material fibrous. Denier is a direct numbering system in which the lower numbers represent the finer sizes and the higher numbers the larger sizes. Glass fibers are the only manufactured fibers that are not measured by denier. A 1-denier nylon is not equal in size to a 1-denier rayon, however, because the fibers differ in density. Tex is equal to the weight in grams of 1,000 meters (one kilometer) of the fibrous material.

Fibers themselves are classified into two major classes: Natural and manufactured. A natural fiber is any fiber that exists as it is in the natural state, such as cotton, wool, or silk. Manufactured fibers are made by processing natural or synthetic organic polymers into a fiber-forming substance; they can be classified as cellulosic or synthetic. Cellulosic fibers are either made from regenerated or derivative cellulosic (fibrous) polymers, such as wood or cotton. Synthetic fibers are formed from substances that, at any point in the manufacturing process, are not a fiber; examples are nylon, polyester, and saran. No nylon or polyester fibers exist in nature and they are made of chemicals put through reactions to produce the fiber-forming substance. The generic names for manufactured and synthetic fibers were established as part of the Textile Fiber Products Identification Act enacted by the U.S. Congress in 1954 (table 5.1).

The process of forensic fiber analysis can be thought of in two-stages— *identification* and *comparison*. Although the methods used in these processes may be similar, the goals of each are quite different. Identification is a process of classification. This involves observing the physical and chemical properties of the fiber that help put it into sets (or classes) with successively smaller memberships. These properties can be observed by a combination of microscopy and chemical analysis. Identification tests are performed prior to comparisons and every effort should be made to conserve fibers for later comparison if the quantity is limited.[14]

Cross-sectional shape, the shape of an individual filament when cut at a right angle to its long axis, is a critical characteristic of fiber analysis. Shapes for manufactured fibers vary by design; there are about 500 different cross-sections currently in use.

Currently, over half of the fibers produced every year are natural fibers and the majority of these are cotton. Natural fibers come from animals, plants, or minerals. Used in many products, it is important for the forensic fiber examiner to have a thorough knowledge of natural fibers and their significance in casework. Animal fibers come either come from mammals (hairs) or from certain invertebrates, such as the silkworm. Animal fibers in textiles are most often from wool-bearing animals, such as sheep and goats, or from fur-bearing animals, such as rabbits, mink, and fox. A comprehensive reference collection is critical to animal hair identifications and comparisons. The microscopic anatomical structures of animal hairs are important to their identification. The three major sources for

Table 5.1   The Textile Fiber Products Identification Act listing of textile fiber definitions

acetate	A manufactured fiber in which the fiber-forming substance is cellulose acetate. Where not less than 92% of the hydroxyl groups are acetylated the term triacetate may be used as a generic description of the fiber.
acrylic	A manufactured fiber in which the fiber-forming substance is any long-chain synthetic polymer composed of at least 85% by weight of acrylonitrile units.
anidex	A manufactured fiber in which the fiber-forming substance is any long-chain synthetic polymer composed of at least 50% by weight of one or more esters of a monohydric alcohol and acrylic acid.
aramid	A manufactured fiber in which the fiber-forming substance is any long-chain synthetic polyamide in which at least 85% of the amide linkages are attached directly to two aromatic rings.
glass	A manufactured fiber in which the fiber-forming substance is glass.
nylon	A manufactured fiber in which the fiber-forming substance is any long-chain synthetic polyamide in which less than 85% of the amide linkages are attached directly to two aromatic rings.
metallic	A manufactured fiber composed of metal, plastic-coated metal, metal-coated plastic, or a core completely covered by metal.
modacrylic	A manufactured fiber in which the fiber-forming substance is any long-chain synthetic polymer composed of less than 85% but at least 35% by weight of acrylonitrile units.
novoloid	A manufactured fiber in which the fiber-forming substance is any long-chain synthetic polymer composed of at least 85% of a long chain polymer of vinylidene dinitrile where the vinylidene dinitrile content is no less than every other unit in the polymer chain.
olefin	A manufactured fiber in which the fiber-forming substance is any long-chain synthetic polymer composed of at least 85% by weight of ethylene, propylene, or other olefin units.
polyester	A manufactured fiber in which the fiber-forming substance is any long-chain synthetic polymer composed of at least 85% by weight of an ester or a substituted aromatic carboxylic acid, including but not restricted to substituted terephthalate units and parasubstituted hydroxybenzoate units.
rayon	A manufactured fiber composed of regenerated cellulose, as well as manufactured fibers composed of regenerated cellulose in which substituents have replaced not more than 15% of the hydrogens of the hydroxyl groups.

(Continued)

Table 5.1 Continued

lyocel	A manufactured fiber composed of precipitated cellulose and produced by a solvent extrusion process where no chemical intermediates are formed.
saran	A manufactured fiber in which the fiber-forming substance is any long-chain synthetic polymer composed of at least 80% by weight of vinylidene chloride units.
spandex	A manufactured fiber in which the fiber-forming substance is any long-chain synthetic polymer composed of at least 85% of a segmented polyurethane.
vinal	A manufactured fiber in which the fiber-forming substance is any long-chain synthetic polymer composed of at least 50% by weight of vinyl alcohol units and in which the total of the vinyl alcohol units and any one or more of the various acetal units is at least 85% by weight of the fiber.
vinyon	A manufactured fiber in which the fiber-forming substance is any long-chain synthetic polymer composed of at least 85% by weight of vinyl chloride units.

fibers derived from plants are the seed, the stem, or the leaf. The most common plant fibers encountered in case work are cotton, flax, and jute.

Manufactured fibers are the various families of fibers produced from fiber-forming substances, which may be synthesized polymers, modified or transformed natural polymers, or glass. Synthetic fibers are those manufactured fibers which are synthesized from chemical compounds (e.g., nylon, polyester). Therefore, all synthetic fibers are manufactured, but not all manufactured fibers are synthetic. Manufactured fibers are formed by extruding a fiber-forming substance, called spinning dope, through a hole or holes in a showerheadlike device called a spinneret; this process is called spinning. The spinning dope is created by rendering solid monomeric material into a liquid or semiliquid form with a solvent or heat.[20] The microscopic characteristics of manufactured fibers are the basic features used to distinguish them. Manufactured fibers differ physically in their optical and chemical properties and appearance.[21]

Optical Properties

Fibers vary in shape but are almost always thicker in the centre than near the edges. Thus they act as crude lenses, either concentrating or dispersing the light that passes through them. This phenomenon is used to determine the fiber's refractive index; refractive index is the ratio of the speed light in a vacuum to the speed of light in a medium, in this case a fiber. Refractive indices for fibers range from 1.46 to over 2.0 for very optically dense fibers such as Kevlar. Another useful trait of a manufactured fiber is its birefringence. Fibers have two optical axes and, because the fibers have an internal orientation (analogous to the grain in wood), each has a different refractive index. Birefringence is the difference between the two indices and ranges from −0.01 to −0.2 or more. Because manufactured fibers vary in their optical density, refractive index and birefringence are useful traits for fiber identification.[22]

Color is one of the most critical characteristics in a fiber comparison. Almost all manufacturing industries are concerned with product appearance. Everything that is manufactured has a color to it and often these colors are imparted to the end product. Particular colors are chosen for some products rather than others (it is difficult to find "safety orange" carpeting, for example) and these colors may indicate the end product. A dye is an organic chemical that is able to absorb and reflect certain wavelengths of visible light. Pigments are microscopic, water-insoluble particles that are either incorporated into the fiber at the time of production or are bonded to the surface of the fiber by a resin. Some fiber types, such as olefins, are not easily dyed and therefore are often pigmented. Over 80 dyers worldwide are registered with the American Association of Textile Chemists and Colorists (AATCC) and almost 350 trademarked dyes are registered with them. Some trademarked dyes have as many as 40 variants. Over 7,000 dyes and pigments are currently produced worldwide. Natural dyes, such as indigo, have been known since before recorded history while synthetic dyes have gained prominence largely since the First World War.[23] Very few textiles are colored with only one dye and even a simple dye may be put through eight to ten processing steps to achieve a final dye form, shade, and strength. When all of these factors are considered, it becomes apparent that it is virtually impossible to dye textiles in a continuous method; that is, dyeing separate batches of fibers or textiles is the rule rather than the exception. This color variability has the potential to be significant in forensic fiber comparisons. The number of producible colors is nearly infinite and color is an easy discriminator.[24]

The most basic method of color analysis is visual examination of single fibers with a comparison microscope. Visual examination and comparison are quick and excellent screening techniques. Because visual examination is a subjective method, it must be used in conjunction with an objective method.

Chemical analysis involves extracting the dye and characterizing or identifying its chemistry. Chemical analysis addresses the type of dye(s) used to color the fiber and may help to sort out metameric colors. It can be difficult to extract the dye from the fiber; however, as forensic samples typically are small and textile dyers take great pains to ensure that the dye stays in the fiber. Dye analysis is also a destructive method, rendering the fiber useless for further color analysis. Yet some fiber have colors so similar that chemical analysis is required to distinguish them.[25]

Instrumental analysis, typically microspectrophotometry, offers the best combinations of strengths and the fewest weaknesses of the three methods outlined. Instrumental readings are objective and repeatable; the results are quantitative and the methods can be standardized. Importantly, it is not destructive to the fiber and the analysis may be repeated. Again, very light fibers may present a problem with weak results and natural fibers may exhibit high variations due to uneven dye uptake.[26]

Chemical Properties

While microscopy offers an accurate method of fiber examination, it is necessary to confirm these observations. Analyzing the fibers chemically may provide additional information about the specific polymer type or types that make up the fiber. For most of the generic polymer classes, various subclasses exist which can assist in discriminating between optically similar fibers. Both Fourier-transform spectroscopy (FTIR) and pyrolysis-gas chromatography (PGC) are methods of assessing the chemical structure of polymers. FTIR is the preferred method because it is nondestructive.[27]

Interpretations

Identifying unknown fibers and comparing them with known fibers is only the first step in a forensic fiber analysis. The second and more critical step is to draw and formulate conclusions about the significance of the association between known and unknown fibers. It is not possible, for example, to tell the difference chemically or optically between two adjacent fibers taken from the same shirt. We know through simple observation that the two fibers came from the same shirt but we cannot prove this to someone who did not see us remove the fibers. Any test we devise for the two fibers and the rest of the fibers in the shirt will yield the same analytical results. Those fibers are different, however, from fibers comprising many, many other shirts; in fact, it is rare to find two fibers at random that exhibit all the same microscopic characteristics and optical properties

It is rare to find unrelated fibers on a particular item and the probability of chance occurrence decreases rapidly as the number of different matching fiber types increases. Frequency studies add to the foundation of fiber transfer interpretation data. For example, one study has calculated the frequency of finding at least one red woolen fiber on a car seat is 5.1%; if more than 5 are found, however, the relative frequency plummets to 1.4%. Quoting the authors of that study, "(e)xcept for blue denim or grey/black cotton, no fiber should be considered as common."[28] One study cross-checked fibers from 20 unrelated cases, looking for incidental positive associations; in over 2 million comparisons, no incidental positive associations were found.[29] This makes fiber evidence very powerful in demonstrating associations.

Paint

The forensic analysis of coatings, encompassing any surface coating intended to protect, aesthetically improve, or provide some special quality, is one of the most complex topics in the forensic laboratory. The manufacture and application of paints and coatings is one of the most complicated areas in industrial chemistry. A forensic paint examiner, even with specialization in that one material, cannot be fully acquainted with the range of coatings and paints used worldwide. This complexity is in the forensic scientist's favor, however, because variety and variation make for a more specific categorization of evidence: more specificity presents the potential for greater evidentiary significance in court.[30]

A paint is a suspension of pigments and additives intended to color or protect a surface. A pigment is fine insoluble powder, whose granules remain intact and are dispersed evenly across a surface. Pigments may be organic, inorganic, or a mixture. The additives in paint come in a dizzying variety but have some constants. The binder is that portion of the coating which allows the pigment to be distributed across the surface. The term "vehicle" typically refers to the solvents, resins, and other additives that form a continuous film, binding the pigment to the surface. If the binder and vehicle sound similar, they are: The terms are sometimes used interchangeably in the coatings industry. Solvents dissolve the binder and give the paint a suitable consistency for application (brushing, spraying, etc.). Once the paint has been applied, the solvent and many of the additives evaporate; a hard polymer film (the binder) containing the dispersed pigment remains to cover and seal the surface.[31, 32]

Paints can be divided into four major categories. The first is architectural paints, which are most often found in residences and businesses. Product coatings, those applied in the manufacture of products including automobiles, are the second major category. Because automobiles play a central role in society and, therefore, in crime, much of this section will focus on automotive paints and coatings. The third kind, special purpose coatings, fulfills specific needs beyond protection or aesthetic improvement, such as skid-resistance, waterproofing, or luminescence (as on the dials of wristwatches). Finally, art paints, are encountered in forgery cases. Modern art paints are similar in many respects to architectural paints but many artists formulate their own paints, leading to potentially unique sources.

The automotive finishing process for vehicles consists of at least four separate coatings. The first is a pretreatment, typically zinc electroplating, applied to the steel body of the vehicle to inhibit rust. The steel is then washed with a detergent, rinsed, treated again, and then washed again. The forensic paint analyst should be aware that any zinc found during elemental analysis may come from this coating and not necessarily the paint itself.

The second coating is a primer, usually an epoxy resin with corrosion-resistant pigments; the color of the primer is coordinated with the final vehicle color to minimize contrast and "bleed through." The steel body of the vehicle is dipped in a large bath of the liquid primer which is plated on by electrical conduction. The primer coating is finished with a powder "primer surfacer" that smoothes the surface of the metal and provides better adhesion for the next coating.

The topcoat is the third coating applied to the vehicle and may be in the form of a single color layer coat, a multilayer coat, or a metallic color coat; this is the layer that most people think of when they think of a vehicle's color. Topcoat chemistry is moving toward water-based chemistries to provide a healthier environment for factory workers and the public; for example, heavy metals, such as lead or chrome, are no longer used in topcoats. Metallic or pearlescent coatings, growing in preference for new vehicles, have small metal or mica flakes incorporated to provide a shimmering, color-changing effect. Metallic pigments, including zinc, nickel, steel, and gold-bronze, give a glittering finish to a vehicle's color while pearlescent pigments, mica chips coated with titanium dioxide and ferric oxide, try to replicate the glowing luster of pearls. The topcoat is often applied and flashed, or partially cured, and then finished with the next and final coating, the clearcoat.

Clearcoats are unpigmented coatings applied to improve gloss and durability of a vehicle's coating. Historically, clearcoats were acrylic-based in their chemistry but nearly half of the automotive manufacturers have moved to two-component urethanes.[33]

A final note on vehicle coloration is that of the newer plastic substrates. Vehicle bodies are no longer made exclusively of steel and various plastics are now commonly used. For example, fenders may be nylon, polymer blends, or polyurethane resins; door panels and hoods may be of thermo-setting polymers; front grills and bumper strips have long been plastic or polymer but now may be colored to match the vehicle. Braking systems, chassis, and even entire cars (BASF unveiled an entirely plastic car in 1999, as an extreme example) are now constructed from plastics. It would not be unusual for the forensic paint examiner to encounter steel, aluminium, and polymer parts on the same vehicle, each colored by a very different coating system.

Analysis of Paint Samples

The initial step in forensic paint analysis is to look at the sample. Often, the first step may be the last: If significant differences are apparent in the known and questioned samples, the analysis is completed and the paints are excluded. The paint samples are described, noting their condition, weathering characteristics, size, shape, exterior colors, and major layers present in each sample. The examiner's notes should include written descriptions, photographs, and drawings, as necessary. Because significant changes can be made to a portion of a sample in the process of preparation and examination, it is crucial to document how that sample was received.

Microscopical comparisons of paint layers can reveal slight variations between samples in color, pigment appearance, flake size and distribution, surface details, inclusions, and layer defects. Any visual comparisons must be done with the samples side by side in the same field of view (or with a comparison microscope), typically at the same magnification. Polarized light microscopy (PLM) is appropriate for the examination of layer structure as well as the comparison and/or identification of particles in a paint film including, but not limited to, pigments, extenders, additives, and contaminants.

Many instrumental methods are available for analyzing the complex chemistry of paints. Rarely will all the instruments listed below appear in a single laboratory—even if they did, the laboratory's analytical scheme would probably not include all of them—and the order of examination will be keyed to the instrumentation at hand.[34]

Infrared spectroscopy (IR) can identify binders, pigments, and additives used in paints and coatings. Most IRs used in forensic science laboratories employ a microscopical bench to magnify the image of the sample and focus the beam on the sample. The bench is a microscope stage attached to the instrument chassis with optics to route the beam through the microscope and back to the detector. Most modern IRs will also be Fourier transform infrared (FT-IR) spectrometers, which employ a mathematical transformation (the fast Fourier transform) which translates the spectral frequency into wavelength.

Pyrolysis gas chromatography (PGC or PyGC) disassembles molecules through heat. It is a destructive technique that uses the breakdown products for comparison of paints and identification of the binder type. PGC is influenced by the size and shape of the samples and instrument parameters, such as rate of heating, the final temperature, the type of column, and gas flow rates. The conditions for one analysis should be the same as those for the next and should be run very close in time to each other. If the instrumentation is available, pyrolysis products may be identified by pyrolysis gas chromatography-mass spectrometry (PGC-MS). The resulting reconstructed total ion chromatogram may help to identify additives, organic pigments, and impurities in addition to binder components.

One of the most generally useful instruments in forensic paint analysis is the scanning electron microscope outfitted with an energy dispersive x-ray spectrometer (SEM/EDS). SEM/EDS can be used to characterize the structure and elemental composition of paint layers. The SEM uses an electron beam rather than a light beam and changes the nature of the information received from the paint. The primary reason for analyzing paint samples with an SEM/EDS system is to determine the elemental composition of the paint and its layers.[35]

Interpretations

Statistically evaluating trace evidence, including paint, is difficult. A consensus of forensic paint examiners agrees that the following factors strengthen an association between two analytically indistinguishable paint samples:

- The number of layers
- The sequence of layers

- The color of each layer
- Cross-transfer of paint between items

Scott Ryland of the Florida Department of Law Enforcement forensic laboratory in Orlando, and his colleagues have stated that an association between two paint samples with six or more correlating layers indicates that the chance that the samples originated from two different sources is "extremely remote."[33] In cases with evidence this strong, merely stating that the two samples "could have had a common origin" is not enough— that level of statement undermines the strength of a six-layer-plus association. Though it is not a statistical or mathematical answer, it does not mean the statement is not accurate, valid, or sound.

The significance of architectural paints varies and is in general not as well documented in the literature. This is most likely due to the enormous variability in colors, application styles, and the application of the paint itself (not all brushstrokes are equal, which results in highly variable layers *between* samples). The situation is similar with spray paints, about which even less is known.

Instances of attempts to generate statistics to assess the evidentiary value of paint have been found in both clinical literature and in casework. These are based, as are most manufacturing inquires, on the concept of a batch lot, a unit of production and sampling that contains a set of analytically indistinguishable products. For example, a batch tank of automotive paint of a given color may hold 500 to 10,000 gallons, which would color between 170 and 1,600 vehicles. This would then be the unit of comparison for the significance of an automotive paint comparison—the manufacturing batch lot. If analytically identifiable differences can be determined between batch lots, the base population is set for any other analytically indistinguishable paint samples. The final significance will be determined by the number of vehicles in the area at the time of the crime and other characteristics that set that sample apart (very rare or very common makes or models). By comparison, a batch lot of architectural paint may be from 100 to 4,500 gallons.[31]

Glass

Glass is defined as an amorphous solid, a hard, brittle usually transparent material without the atomic organization (a crystal lattice) found in most other solids. Glass consists of doped oxides of silicon: The silicon oxides come from sand, the doping comes from other materials that provide useful properties. The sand is melted with the other desired ingredients and then allowed to cool without crystallizing. The glass may be cooled in a mold or through a process that allows the glass to become flat.

There are three major types of glass encountered as forensic evidence: sheet or flat glass, container glass, and glass fibers. Flat glass is used to make windows and windshields; it can also be shaped into various forms, such as light bulbs. Container glass is used to make bottles and drinking glasses. Glass fibers are found in fiberglass and fiber optic cables as well as composite materials. Specialty glass, like optical glass used to make eyeglass lenses, may be encountered in forensic cases although less frequently. More than 700 types of glass are in use today in the United States and the frequency of occurrence relates to the prevalence of specific products. For example, more bottle or window glass, on average, would be encountered than optical or specialty glass. Unless a fracture or physical is possible, small pieces of glass are considered to be class evidence.[36, 37]

Types of Glass

Float glass is made by mixing sand, limestone, soda ash, dolomite, iron oxide, and salt cake and melting the mix in a large furnace. Pure silicon glass is rarely used as it is. Instead, specific amounts of various impurities that alter the final properties in a predictable fashion are added (called doping) to the melted glass. For instance, sodium carbonate (Na_2CO_3, or soda) is added to make the glass melt at a lower temperature and viscosity. This makes it more malleable. Calcium oxide (CaO, or lime), as another example, stabilizes the glass and makes it less soluble. If both calcium oxide and sodium carbonate are added, the glass is called soda-lime glass. Boron oxide (B_2O_3) makes glass highly heat-resistant; the result is borosilicate glass, better known through one of its product names as Pyrex[©]. Borosilicate glass appears in cookware, thermometers, and laboratory glassware.

The molten glass is fed into a bath of molten tin through a controlled gate, called a tweel. A pressurized atmosphere of nitrogen and hydrogen is maintained to eliminate oxygen and to prevent oxidation of the tin to prevent the tin from oxidizing. Some tin is absorbed into the glass, and, under ultraviolet light, the tin side can be differentiated from the nontin side. As the glass flows down the tin bath, the temperature is slowly reduced so that it anneals without internal strain or visible cracks.

The glass is cut by machines into manageable sized pieces. Surface tension, flow, and the tin bath cause the glass to form with an even thickness and a smooth glossy surface on both sides.

Glass may be strengthened by tempering or annealing, where the glass surface is intentionally stressed through heating and rapid cooling. Tempered glass breaks into many small solid pieces, instead of sharp shards; it is used in car windows for this reason. Windscreens in the Unites States are not tempered glass but are two layers of glass that sandwich a layer of plastic. When the windscreen breaks, the plastic keeps the glass from spraying the passenger compartment.

It is generally accepted that glass can be individualized when it breaks into pieces that have at least one intact edge that can be fitted to the edge of another piece; this is called a physical or fracture match, for obvious reasons. Glass is hard and brittle, so it does not deform when broken; glass is amorphous, so there are no lattice points along which the molecules would regularly separate when subjected to force Glass fractures are random events and no two pieces of similar glass would be expected to break in exactly the same pattern. If two pieces of glass have a mechanical fit, the conclusion is made that they were once part of the same piece of glass. This conclusion is often strengthened by stress marks along the face of the broken glass edge. Stress marks are microscopic lines randomly generated by the propagation of force along breaking fracture.[36, 37]

The majority of forensic glass samples consists of particles too small to be physically matched and, therefore, are class evidence. The analysis of glass fragments is based on the optical properties and elemental content of the material. The first step, however, is to determine that the fragments are glass and not some other material. Glass is differentiated from other similar materials by its hardness, structure, and behavior when exposed to polarized light. Glass can be differentiated from translucent plastic, for example, by pressing it with a needle point: most plastics are indented by the needle but glass is not. Table salt, as another example, exhibits cubic crystals; glass is amorphous and does not. Glass is isotropic, meaning it has the same properties in all directions; most translucent minerals are anisotropic (think of them as having an optical "grain," much like a wood grain). Anisotropic materials display birefringence, or double refraction, because their "grain" changes the properties of the light that passes through it. Glass, being isotropic, has no birefringence.[38, 39]

Once it is determined that the material is glass, preliminary tests for similarity, including color, surface characteristics, flatness, thickness, and fluorescence, must be conducted. If the two samples are different at any stage, then they are excluded as not having come from the same piece of glass.

Refraction occurs when light passes through a transparent medium: the light is bent away from its original path and is impeded by the medium's optical density. Glass exhibits refraction. The amount of refraction caused by glass is an important physical property for the comparison of known and unknown exhibits. The refractive index of a material is the ratio of the velocity of light in a vacuum (or air) to the velocity as it passes through the medium. Refractive index is always greater than 1.0 because light travels fastest in a vacuum. The range of refractive indices for glass is between 1.4 and 1.7 and different glasses have different refractive indices, making this property valuable in distinguishing between glass fragments. It is not possible to measure the refractive index of glass directly; rather it must be indirectly determined through a phenomenon called the Becke line. The glass fragment acts as a crude lens and, when the piece of glass is taken out of focus (by increasing the distance from the bottom of the lens to the top of the fragment), light will either be focused out of or into the fragment depending on the refractive index of the surrounding medium. The band of light—the Becke line—thus focused moves toward the medium of higher refractive index; if the glass has a higher refractive index than the surrounding medium, for example, the Becke line will move *into* the glass. A series of liquids of known refractive index (to three decimal places) can be used in a high/low pattern until the glass fragment disappears in the liquid signaling that they have the same refractive index (the glass and the liquid are bending the light to the same degree).[39, 40]

The amounts of specific elements in glass can assist in characterizing its source. Manufacturers control the concentrations of certain elements so that a particular glass product has the intended end-use properties. Depending on the elements and quality controls in manufacturing, these concentrations can help to identify the product type of a glass fragment. Glass manufacturers typically do not control for trace element concentrations, however, unless these would adversely effect the physical or optical properties of the glass. The differences in concentrations of manufacturer-controlled elements or uncontrolled trace elements may be used to differentiate sources when the variation among objects exceeds the variation within each object.[41] Element concentrations may be used to differentiate among

- glasses made by different manufacturers;
- glasses from different production lines of a single manufacturer;

- specific production runs of glass from a single manufacturer; and
- (occasionally) individual glass objects produced at the same production facility.

Soils

Soil is underutilized as forensic evidence. Even forensic scientists who should know better may shrug and say, "It's all dirt." Nothing could be further from the truth. In a way, forensic soil analysis has been "forgotten" as it has a long and practical history. A notable early forensic soil case occurred in 1908 in Bavaria.[42] A local man of "low reputations" named Schlicter, previously suspected of criminal activity, was suspected of murdering Margarethe Filbert. Georg Popp, who was to become a pioneer in forensic microscopy and trace evidence, was asked to examine the evidence. Popp found thickly caked soil on the sole of the suspect's shoes in front of the heel; Schlicter's wife testified that she had cleaned and polished those dress shoes just before he wore them. Popp reasoned that the soil must have been deposited on the shoe the last time Schlicter had worn the shoes, which happened to be the day of the murder. Also, Popp reasoned that the layers of soil on the shoes represented a sequential deposit, with the earliest material deposited directly on the leather, in accordance with the concept of superimposition offered by Charles Lyell. Popp's careful examination revealed a distinct sequence of layers:

1. On the leather: A layer of goose droppings
2. Grains of red sandstone on top of the goose droppings
3. A mixture of coal, brick dust, and cement fragments

Popp compared all three layers on the shoe with soil from the suspect's home, the scene of the crime, and the castle where the suspect's gun was found. Schlicher claimed he had walked through his own fields on that day. Tellingly, no fragments of porphyry with milky quartz—rocks which were found in the sample from the suspect's fields—were found on Schlicter's shoes. Popp demonstrated that two samples from the shoes compared with two places associated with the crime and that the sequence of events was consistent with the theory of the crime, and that Schlicter's alibi was not supported by the evidence. Many crimes like Schlicter's could be solved today if forensic scientists paid more attention to soil analysis.[43, 44]

Soil is a mixture of organic material and minerals. The organic matter comes from dead plants and animals while many of the minerals come from the rocks underground. Because plants grow on top of the soil and the rocks are found underground, soil is layered. It takes thousands of years for rock to develop through weathering and hundreds of years for rich organic layers to build up to create soil. Many soils are comprise entirely transported weathered material (flooding, dust fall, etc.). Human activity also affects soil. People alter soils by adding natural or synthetic materials or fertilizer to make them more suitable for plant growth. Drainage and water-retaining capacity, for landscaping or construction, also affect the quality of the soil. The depletion of nutrients, pollution, soil contamination, soil compaction, and the rate of erosion, all affect soil composition and content. The proportions and types of minerals and organic matter help determine the characteristics of a particular soil.[45]

The majority of the solid portion of soil is mineral particles. Organic matter makes up about 5% to 10% of the volume of soil; DNA testing on the organic fraction of soil may eventually yield useful forensic data.

Mineral particles are divided into three groups based on their size: Clay (<0.002 mm), silt (0.002 to 0.05 mm), and sand (0.05 to 2.0 mm). The proportion of particles from each group determines the soil texture. For example, a loam has equivalent amounts of all three particle types. A sandy loam is higher in sand; a clay loam is higher in clay. Soil structure, or how soil is put together, can be as important as what it is made of. Most soil particles are held together in aggregates of many particles. The size and stability of these aggregates determine the size of pores. Soils vary widely in composition and structure both horizontally and vertically.[45]

Forensic geologists look at soil differently than agriculturalists or soil scientists: they are concerned with the transfer of soil particles from one location or object to another, either accidentally or purposefully. The goal of forensic soil analysis is to associate soil found at a crime scene or on a victim or suspect to its source. The forensic geologist measures and compares those physical and chemical properties that distinguish two soil samples or indicate that they could have originated from the same location.[43]

Questioned soil samples are accidental: A murderer rarely chooses the best sample of soil for his shoe sole or tire tread when transporting a body. The ad hoc crime sample, then, may lack some of the total population of particles present at the scene. Therefore, questioned samples can never be expected to be identical to a known sample, which should be representative of the location from which it came. The forensic examiner thus can only study the particles in the known sample that are the same size as those in the questioned sample. Known samples should be collected as close as possible to the site where the questioned material is thought to have originated.

The physical properties of soil are easy and inexpensive to measure and are conservative of sample. Standard methods of soil analysis are available from the American Society of Testing and Materials and the U.S. Geological Survey. The most common physical tests of soil are color and particle size distribution. Moisture content, mineral distribution, and location, all affect soil color—dry soils tend to be light tan or white, for example, and agricultural soils tend to be dark brown because of their high organic content. The healthy human eye is very good at comparing soil sample color; standard color charts and systems, such as the Munsell Color System, are available to help determine colors more objectively.

The polarizing light microscope is the best tool to identify the mineral component of soil. Particle analysis is key to understanding the composition of the samples. The Particle Atlas is an indispensable tool for polarized light microscopy of particles and minerals. The basic method of determining soil particle size is by sieving. A soil sample is weighed, dried, run through a nested series of sieves. Each fraction is weighed and the individual particles are examined; the percentage of each particle size range is calculated. Individual particles are then examined for their optical and, in some cases, chemical properties with the polarizing light microscope; refractive indices, birefringence, and other optical traits are used to identify mineral and organic particles in a soil sample.

The scanning electron microscope (SEM) is a powerful tool in the analysis of soils. Surface information, atomic weights, and elemental composition (to parts per million) can be produced from a single examination. Magnifications of up to 250,000 are possible allowing for the analysis of very small particles.

CHAPTER **6**

DNA

September 11, O.J. Simpson, President Clinton, and The Unknown Solider all have at least one thing in common: Forensic DNA analysis. The impact forensic DNA typing has had on our modern society can hardly be overstated. It has even affected our perceptions of *past* societies—witness the revelation that Thomas Jefferson may have fathered a child with one of his slaves. DNA typing has been and continues to be a disruptive technology in the forensic and natural sciences, changing the way everything works. Advances in DNA analysis have not only allowed for personal identification from biologic material but have greatly increased the kinds of biological material that can be analyzed. Discovered in 1984 by Sir Alec Jeffreys, DNA typing (often erroneously called "DNA fingeprinting") heralded a new era in forensic science and genetic research. But actually Jeffreys was doing forensic research at the time. "I had been working on disease genes," Jeffreys told the *Observer*, "The last thing I was thinking about was paternity suits or forensics. But I would have had to have been a complete idiot not to spot the implications."[1] The application of DNA typing to forensic science, and, indeed, to all of biology, has come far since Jeffreys' original discovery.

Deoxyribonucleic acid (DNA) is a polymer, a molecule made of smaller repeating units called monomers. DNA is present in nearly all living cells except in red blood cells and nerve cells. Forensic science uses two types of DNA: Nuclear and mitochondrial. Nuclear DNA resides in the nucleus of the cell and contains the information for growth and maintenance of that cell's functions. Mitochondrial DNA resides in a subunit of active cells, called the mitochondrion, that play a role in energy production for the cell. As well as having different functions in life, these DNAs have different applications in forensic analyses.

One of the applications of DNA testing is that it not only helps to convict but also serves to exonerate. A 1995 survey of laboratories reported 20 to 25% of the cases.[2] Before the advent of DNA testing these suspects might have been indicted and possibly been convicted on the basis of weak or misguided evidence. Many wrongful imprisonments have been discovered through efforts such as the Innocence Project, which helps obtain postconviction DNA testing for those who feel they were wrongly convicted. More than 189 convictions in the United States have been vacated on the basis of DNA results. Postconviction testing is requested not only in cases in which DNA testing was never done but also in cases in which newer technologies may now be able to provide a definitive answer. For example, in June of 1996, Kevin Lee Green was released after being convicted by a jury of beating his wife and killing the fetus she carried. Green was released when DNA tests confirmed the confession of a second man to five other unsolved homicides from almost 20 years earlier. Green had been in prison for 17 years.[3, 4]

Nuclear DNA

Human nuclear DNA (so called because it is found in the nucleus of the cell) is arranged into 46 structures called chromosomes (figure 6.1). The chromosomes are paired, resulting in 23 total pairs; one arm of each chromosome pair comes from the father and the other comes from the mother. Sperm contain 23 chromosomes as does the ovum; when the sperm fertilizes the egg, the 23 chromosomal arms from both pair up and form the 46 chromosomes found in every nucleated cell in the offspring.

The molecules of nuclear DNA have a double-helix structure; think of a ladder twisted about its central axis. The poles of the ladder are the same for all organisms and are made of alternating sugar molecules (deoxyribose) and phosphates. Each sugar molecule has one of four bases, called nucleotides, attached to it; these are adenine (A), guanine (G), cytosine (C) and thymine (T). These bases bond to other bases in a specific pattern: Adenine and thymine always pair together and guanine and cytosine do the same with each other. Nuclear DNA molecules, therefore, consist of sugar-phosphate poles with base-pair rungs (A-T, T-A, G-C or C-G). The base-pair rungs along the ladder can occur in any order. The order of the base pairs constitutes a language of sorts, a code, for translating DNA into the proteins, processes,

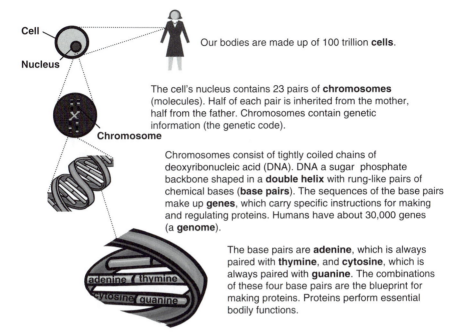

Cell

Nucleus

Our bodies are made up of 100 trillion **cells**.

The cell's nucleus contains 23 pairs of **chromosomes** (molecules). Half of each pair is inherited from the mother, half from the father. Chromosomes contain genetic information (the genetic code).

Chromosome

Chromosomes consist of tightly coiled chains of deoxyribonucleic acid (DNA). DNA a sugar phosphate backbone shaped in a **double helix** with rung-like pairs of chemical bases (**base pairs**). The sequences of the base pairs make up **genes**, which carry specific instructions for making and regulating proteins. Humans have about 30,000 genes (a **genome**).

The base pairs are **adenine**, which is always paired with **thymine**, and **cytosine**, which is always paired with **guanine**. The combinations of these four base pairs are the blueprint for making proteins. Proteins perform essential bodily functions.

adenine thymine
cytosine guanine

Figure 6.1   An overview of human DNA

and functions of a living cell. It is all very well to know that "ndtuhqirkcepdfjuzxmeeedorrelayboothwovg" is present but it does not make any sense until the order is correct: "The quick red fox jumped over the lazy brown dog."

Each strand of DNA is sectioned into areas called genes. The sequence of base pairs in each gene codes for a specific thing, much as the sequence of letters forms a word. The ordering of the base pairs in genes provides the manufacturing instructions for the various proteins in the body. Each gene codes for a particular protein. Nearly all the nuclear DNA in our bodies (>99%) is the same from for one person as the next; that is, it codes for the things that make us a species. The remaining less than 1% carries genetic information that makes one human being different from another. Some traits are coded for by one gene but most traits are coded for by many genes, often on multiple chromosomes. Many traits exist in alternate forms, called alleles; eye color is a good example. Each person will inherit one allele from their mother and one from their father. All the alleles for a trait are typically found at one location on a gene, called a locus (Latin for "place"). High allelic variation at a specific locus or loci provides the basis for DNA typing.

Alleles vary in two ways. The first is sequence polymorphisms, where a single base- pair change occurs which alters the sequence.

C T C G A T T A A G G   C T C G G T T A A G G
G A G C T A A T T C C   G A G C C A A T T C C

Notice that the base *pair* changes and only one base. The two sequences of double stranded DNA are exactly the same except at the location in bold. The other form of allelic variation is called length polymorphism. For example, consider the variation displayed below:

Four score and seven years ago

Four score and and seven years ago

Four score and and and seven years ago

Four score and and and and seven years ago

These phrases are the same except for the repeating "and." Now consider the length polymorphism that occurs in the following DNA sequences:

(1) C A T G T A C - C A T G T A C
    G T A C A T G - G T A C A T G
(2) C A T G T A C - C A T G T A C - C A T G T A C - C A T G T A C
    G T A C A T G - G T A C A T G - G T A C A T G - G T A C A T G

Both these consist of a seven base-pair sequence that is repeated; (1) is repeated twice, the (2) is repeated four times. Because the repeats are next to each other, without any different base pairs in between, these are referred to as tandem repeats. If these repeats are found at the same locus in different people or in the same person, then this locus is described as having a variable number of tandem repeats (VNTRs).[5]

How It Is Analyzed

The first step in the analytical process is extracting DNA from the known sample, typically a swabbing of cheek cells or drawn blood, and questioned samples from the suspect, victim, or crime scene, such as blood, semen, or other body fluids. Successful DNA typing relies on isolating DNA of sufficient quantity, quality, and purity to yield an adequate DNA profile. For some samples, sufficient DNA without contaminants can be extracted; for others, the environmental destruction may have been so great that no usable DNA is available for typing.[6] Crime scenes are not good environments to preserve DNA. Temperature, humidity, bacteria, and other factors can effect the quality of DNA. DNA recovered from evidence or crime scenes may be present in minute quantities or be degraded. This makes it difficult or even impossible to analyze the DNA. As the DNA degrades, it falls apart into smaller and smaller pieces. Early DNA analysis methods were limited in the amount of degradation they could handle—they required long strands of intact DNA. In the early 1990s, Dr. Kary Mullins developed a method replicated a strand of DNA into millions of faithful copies of itself. The method, called polymerase chain reaction (PCR), allowed for the analysis of very small samples of biological material by producing sufficient DNA for analysis. This revolutionary product, for which Mullins was awarded a Nobel Prize in 1993, changed the necessary size of a biological simple from the diameter of a U.S. quarter to the period at the end of this sentence.[5] Because PCR replicates any and all of the DNA contained in an evidence sample, greater attention to contamination issues is necessary when identifying, collecting, and preserving DNA evidence. This is particularly true in the investigation of unsolved cases in which evidence might have been improperly collected or stored.[7]

The current method for forensic DNA analysis takes advantage of sequences of short strands of DNA that repeat in tandem at specific loci that are found on nuclear DNA. These short tandem repeats, or STRs, occur at various loci throughout human DNA. The variable nature of the STR regions that are analyzed for forensic testing increases the discrimination between one DNA profile and another. For example, the likelihood that any two individuals (except identical twins) will have the same 13-loci DNA profile can be as high as 1 in 1 billion or greater.[7] The Federal Bureau of Investigation (FBI) has chosen 13 specific STR loci to serve as the standard for forensic DNA databases. The core set of STR loci standardizes the data structure for all forensic laboratories to establish uniform DNA databases.

Population Genetics

The population frequency ranges for each allele at each locus are known. Using the rule of multiplication, the population frequencies for all of the alleles can be calculated. In DNA analysis, locations on the gene that are polymorphic (more than one type) are purposely chosen.

These loci exhibit variation among members of a population and the more variation that occurs at a locus, the more specific the result will be. For example, in the ABO blood system, type A blood is present in about 42% of the Caucasian population, type O is present in about 43%, type B about 10% and type AB in about 5%. Although variation exists, it is not very discriminating—even the rarest form eliminates only 95% of the Caucasian population. That may sound like as if it would be useful, but in a population of 10 million people, half a million people would have the same blood type.

Forensic DNA analysis uses multiple loci and, where several alleles exist at a particular locus, the frequency of occurrence can be determined for each allele. The frequency of occurrence of *all* of these alleles can be determined by multiplying their individual frequencies because they are considered independent of each other. The 13 STR loci are noncoding regions, that is, they are not known to code for specific traits, such as height, eye color, or propensity for disease. The loci were chosen specifically for their variation and trait neutrality.

Thirteen loci may not seem like many but with the multiplication of their individual frequencies, large numbers soon result. The example of a coin toss may help. On a fair coin, the frequency of occurrence for heads is 0.5 (50%) because only two equally probable outcomes exist: heads and tails. If two coins are tossed, the frequency of occurrence for *two* heads (both coins coming up heads) is 0.25 (25%), 0.5 × 0.5. The frequency of occurrence for three heads from three coins is 0.125, and so on. The multiplication rule works only if the probability of each event is independent of the other events. In genetics, the occurrence of each allele must be independent of all of the other alleles being measured. The multiplication rule can yield gene types that are so rare that the chances of finding more than one person at random within a population with the same genetic makeup are essentially zero.

The probability of having a DNA type from all the 13 loci is extremely small—about one in several billion or even trillion. Given that the U.S. population now exceeds 300 million, the chance of any two people at random having the same exact DNA at all 13 loci is very, very remote. The chance of a random match between two people at all 13 STR loci is one in 3.8 *quadrillion*. "Quadrillion" is what comes after trillion (which is what comes after billion). One quadrillion is a "1" followed by 15 zeros, or

1,000,000,000,000,000,000

To put this into perspective, compared with the world population,

3.8,000,000,000,000,000,000   13 STR random match probability
6,000,000,000,000   World population

This number is accepted by some forensic laboratories as being sufficiently large to constitute individualization. Other laboratories do not accept this and report out the statistics as numbers—just very large numbers.

Mitochondrial DNA (mtDNA)

Not all human DNA is located in the cell's nucleus. Just as bodies have organs, so do cells; they are called organelles ("little organs") and they exist in the cell but outside the nucleus. Some organelles have their own packets of DNA; one of these is the mitochondria (the singular is mitochondrion). Mitochondria function for cells much like our lungs do for us—they help us remove processed gasses and remove waste. The proteins that control these functions are manufactured according to a genetic code separate from that in the nucleus that is housed within the mitochondria.

There are a number of differences between mitochondrial DNA (or mtDNA, for short) and genomic DNA. Mitochondrial DNA is circular in shape, unlike the twisted double ladder of genomic DNA. Mitochondrial DNA is also smaller than genomic DNA but has thousands of copies of mtDNA in each mitochondrion. Only a few copies of genomic DNA exist in a human cell nucleus. Mitochondrial DNA contains a noncoding region of 1,100 base pairs. This region does not code for any particular proteins; it acts as a "spacer" for the sequence. Within this noncoding region, two areas are highly variable in their sequences (so-called hypervariable regions). During a cell's reproduction of DNA, certain base pairs in these hypervariable regions will not be replicated exactly; it is the spacing that is important to the replication, not the sequence itself. Many differences will exist, therefore, between mtDNA from two unrelated people.

One of the most important differences between mtDNA and nuclear DNA is that all mtDNA comes from the mother and none comes from the father. Every descendent of a particular woman should have the same mtDNA sequence, barring mutations. This makes mtDNA very powerful for tracing generations of a family through the maternal side of the family. However, mtDNA often shows a high degree of variation between unrelated people also, making it a powerful tool in forensic typing as well. Some sequences appear the same between nonmaternally related people but this is a very, very small percentage of the population.

Mitochondrial DNA can be the last, best hope to identify people. A very hardy molecule, mtDNA survives in numerous quantities in hairs, bone, and teeth. Often, these are the only remains of individuals who are badly decomposed or are victims of mass disasters, such as plane crashes or bombings. Not all forensic science laboratories that perform genomic DNA analysis also do mtDNA analysis. Those that do generally use DNA sequencing; they determine the entire base pair sequence in the two hypervariable regions of the mtDNA, rather than relying on length polymorphism.

The advent of forensic mtDNA in the mid 1990s heralded a new era of biological analysis in law enforcement. This was especially true for hairs, as it offered a way to add information to microscopic hair examinations. The microscopic comparison of human hairs has been accepted scientifically and legally for decades. Mitochondrial DNA sequencing added another test for assessing the significance of attributing a hair to an individual. Neither the microscopic nor molecular analysis alone, or together, provides positive identification. The two methods complement each other in the information they provide. For example, mtDNA typing can often distinguish between hairs from different sources although they have similar, or insufficient, microscopic hair characteristics. Hair comparisons with a microscope, however, can often distinguish between samples from maternally related individuals where mtDNA analysis is "blind."

In a recent study, the results of microscopic and mitochondrial examinations of human hairs submitted to the FBI Laboratory for analysis were reviewed. Of 170 hair examinations, there were 80 microscopic associations; importantly, only 9 were excluded by mtDNA. Also, 66 hairs that were considered either unsuitable for microscopic examinations or yielded inconclusive microscopic associations were analyzable with mtDNA. Only 6 of these hairs did not provide enough mtDNA and another 3 yielded inconclusive results. This study demonstrates the strength of combining the two techniques.[8]

An example of this usefulness is a case from Florida involving the abduction, sexual assault, and murder of a nine-year-old girl.[9] Among the numerous evidence types encountered in that case (trash bags, fibers, and animal hairs) was a lone hair stuck to the young girl's thigh. The hair had characteristics that made it appear pubiclike but not enough to define *as* pubic. One thing was certain, however: The hair was not that of the young victim. Body hairs, especially pubic hairs, are a product of puberty and the hormones that flood the body during that phase of development. The victim, being prepubescent, could not have produced a hair with those traits. That information, gained through a microscopic examination of the hair, led to the hair being tested for mitochondrial DNA. The sequence of the hair was the same as that of the suspect in the case. Added to the other evidence stacked against him, he ultimately confessed to his brutal crime.

Databases

The Combined DNA Information System (CODIS) is a computer network that connects forensic DNA laboratories at the local, state, and national levels. DNA database systems that use CODIS contain two main criminal indices and a missing persons index. When a DNA profile is developed from crime scene evidence and entered into the forensic (crime scene) index of CODIS, the database software searches thousands of convicted offender DNA profiles (contained in the offender index) of individuals convicted of offenses such as rape and murder. Similar to the Automated Fingerprint Identification System (AFIS), CODIS can aid investigations by efficiently comparing a DNA profile generated from biological evidence left at a crime scene with convicted offender DNA profiles and forensic evidence from other cases contained in CODIS. CODIS can also aid investigations by searching the missing persons index, which contains DNA profiles of unidentified remains and DNA profiles of relatives of those who are missing. Because of the recidivistic nature of violent offenders, the power of a DNA database system is evident not only in the success of solving crimes previously thought unsolvable, but also perhaps more importantly, through the prevention of crime.

The use of DNA evidence and convicted offender DNA databases has expanded significantly since the first U.S. DNA database was created in 1989. Although state and local DNA databases established in the early 1990s contained only DNA profiles from convicted murderers and sex offenders, the undeniable success of DNA databases has resulted in a national trend toward database expansion. All states require at least some convicted offenders to provide a DNA sample to be collected for DNA profiling and, in the year 2000, the Federal Government began requiring certain offenders convicted of Federal or military crimes to also provide a DNA sample for the criminal DNA database. Recognizing that the effectiveness of the DNA database relies on the volume of data contained in both the forensic index (crime scene samples) and the convicted offender index of CODIS, many States are changing their database statutes to include less violent criminals. Many states are enacting legislation to require all convicted felons to submit a DNA profile to the state database. The tendency for states to include all convicted felons in their databases dramatically increases the number of convicted offender DNA profiles against which forensic DNA evidence can be compared, thus making the database system a more powerful tool for law enforcement.

CODIS uses two indices to generate investigative leads in crimes for which biological evidence is recovered from a crime scene. The convicted offender index contains DNA profiles of individuals convicted of crimes ranging from certain misdemeanors to sexual assault and murder. Each state has different "qualifying offenses" for which persons convicted of them must submit a biological sample for inclusion in the DNA database. The forensic index contains DNA profiles obtained from crime scene evidence, such as semen, saliva, or blood. CODIS uses computer software to automatically search across these indices for a potential match. A match made between profiles in the forensic index can link crime scenes to each other, possibly identifying serial offenders. Based on these "forensic hits," police in multiple jurisdictions or states can coordinate their respective investigations and share leads they have developed independent of each other. Matches made between the forensic and convicted offender indices can provide investigators with the identity of a suspect(s). It is important to note that if an "offender hit" is obtained, that information typically is used as probable cause to obtain a new DNA sample from that suspect so the match can be confirmed by the crime laboratory before an arrest is made.

CODIS is implemented as a distributed database with three hierarchical levels (or tiers)—local, state, and national. All three levels contain forensic and convicted offender indices and a population file (used to generate statistics). The hierarchical design provides State and local laboratories with the flexibility to configure CODIS to meet their specific legislative and technical needs.

CODIS works on three levels. Typically, the Local DNA Index System (LDIS) installed at crime laboratories is operated by police departments or sheriffs' offices. DNA profiles originated at the local level can be transmitted to the state and national levels. Each state has a designated laboratory that operates the state DNA Index System (SDIS); this is the second level. SDIS allows local laboratories within that state to compare DNA profiles. SDIS also is the communication path between the local and national tiers. SDIS is typically operated by the agency responsible for implementing and monitoring compliance with the state's convicted offender statute. The third level, the National DNA Index System (NDIS), is the highest level of the CODIS hierarchy and enables qualified State laboratories that are actively participating in CODIS to compare DNA profiles. NDIS is maintained by the FBI under the authority of the DNA Identification Act of 1994.

Cold Cases and Postconviction Testing

A "cold" case is one in which the active investigative leads have hit obstacles or dead ends and slowed the investigation so much that it has stopped. Every law enforcement department throughout the country has unsolved cases that could potentially be aided through forensic DNA analysis. In Austin, Texas, for example, an investigator who read about the potential for obtaining DNA evidence from the ligature used to strangle a victim requested DNA testing on the phone cord used to choke the victim in his case. The attacker attempted to avoid identification by wearing both a condom and rubber gloves. A reliable DNA profile nevertheless was developed from the evidence—during the attack, the criminal had used one hand to hold the victim, leaving only one hand to choke her with the phone cord, so he held the remaining end of the cord with his mouth. Skin cells from his mouth were deposited on the phone cord. The DNA not only solved the Austin case but the perpetrator was linked by DNA to a similar sexual assault in Waco. Such cold hits are becoming an increasingly important aspect of forensic investigations. If one search can solve two crimes, as in the Texas example, think what could be done with all of the cold cases currently unsolved.[10]

Backlogs, however, hinder the potential of DNA databases. The bottleneck created by the surplus of unworked cases presents a dilemma for the criminal justice system: How many criminals, especially recidivists, are still at large because evidence from crimes they have committed remains incomplete? In 2002 (the latest data available), over 500,000 requests for forensic services were outstanding; in the same year the backlogs *doubled* for the largest 50 forensic laboratories in the United States. To achieve a 30-day turn-around time, a Bureau of Justice Statistics reported that laboratories estimated it would take an additional 1,900 employees (at a cost of $70 million) and over $500 million in capital investments.[11]

These statistics ignore the cost of training those new employees—the $70 million is just one year's salaries based on entry level job descriptions. Many more resources need to be provided to the nation's forensic laboratories before they can reach their full potential to contribute to American justice.

Postconviction testing is one way in which forensic DNA analysis is meeting that potential. Those wrongly convicted have recourse to DNA testing to prove their innocence. For example, twice in July 1984, an assailant broke into an apartment, severed phone wires, sexually assaulted a woman, searched through her belongings, and took money and other items. On August 1, 1984, Ronald Cotton was arrested for these crimes. In January 1985, Cotton was convicted by a jury of one count of rape and one count of burglary. In a second trial, in November 1987, Cotton was convicted of both rapes and two counts of burglary. Cotton was sentenced to life plus 54 years. The prosecutor's evidence at trial included a photo identification made by one of the victims, a police lineup identification made by one of the victims, a flashlight found in Cotton's home that resembled the one used by the assailant, and rubber from Cotton's tennis shoe that was consistent with rubber found at one of the crime scenes.

On appeal, the North Carolina Supreme Court overturned the 1985 conviction because the second victim had picked another man out of the lineup and the trial court had not allowed this evidence to be heard by the jury. In November 1987, Cotton was retried, this time for both rapes because the second victim decided that Cotton was her assailant. Before the second trial, a man in prison, who had been convicted for similar crimes similar, told another inmate that he had committed the crimes for which Cotton had been convicted. A superior court judge refused to allow this information into evidence, and Cotton was convicted of both rapes. The next year, Cotton's appellate defender filed a brief but did not argue the failure to admit the second suspect's confession, and the conviction was affirmed.

In 1994, the chief appellate defender requested that two new lawyers take over Cotton's defense. They filed a motion for appropriate relief on the grounds of inadequate appeal counsel. They also filed a motion for DNA testing that was granted in October 1994. In the spring of 1995, the Burlington Police Department turned over all evidence that contained the assailant's semen for DNA testing.

The samples from one victim were too deteriorated to be conclusive, but the samples from the other victim's vaginal swab and underwear were subjected to PCR-based DNA testing and showed no match to Cotton. At the defense's request, the results were sent to the State Bureau of Investigation's DNA database, containing the DNA patterns of convicted violent felons in North Carolina prisons. The state's database showed a match with the convict who had earlier confessed to the crime.

When the DNA test results were reported in May 1995, the district attorney and the defense motioned to dismiss all charges. On June 30, 1995, Cotton was officially cleared of all charges and released from prison. In July 1995, the governor of North Carolina officially pardoned Cotton, making him eligible for $5,000 compensation from the state. Cotton had served 10.5 years of his sentence. Arising from this case is the incredible story of Jennifer Thompson, the victim who had identified Cotton. An aspiring college student at the time of the crime, she made it her purpose to study the assailant's face so that he would be brought to justice. She identified the wrong man. Today, Ms. Thompson speaks out about her experiences and the dangers of relying solely on single eyewitness testimony to convict.*

To date, 184 people have been exonerated through the use of postconviction DNA testing. Innocence Project offices, modeled after the original at Cardozo Law School in New York, are now open in many states. The Innocence Project of West Virginia, at West Virginia University, provides resources for case reviews of all types of evidence, not just DNA; currently, the Project is limited to those convicted of homicides in West Virginia. While it is certainly a travesty of justice to have a person wrongly convicted, it is compounded by the actual criminal potentially being at large. To ensure accuracy in the nation's justice system, more resources need to be made available for postconviction testing.[2]

Mass Disasters and Missing Persons

In the United States, the medical examiner (ME) or coroner generally has the statutory responsibility and authority to identify the deceased and issue a death certificate. The ME must decide whether the forensic information available justifies declaring an identification and signing a death certificate. The consequences of a misidentification can have emotional and legal ramifications. Methods of identification include recognition and comparison of distinguishable physical attributes or personal effects,

---

*For more information on cases like this, visit the Innocence Project website at www.innocenceproject.org.

forensic anthropology, fingerprints, dental records, x-ray records, and, of course, DNA. DNA typing, however, has advantages over other identification methods in some mass fatality situations. DNA analysis can be used even when recovered human remains are quite small and, often, DNA typing is the best technique for reassociating severely fragmented remains. The downside is that DNA typing requires more time, effort, and technology than the traditional identification methods. Mass fatalities with intact bodies may not need DNA to make most of the identifications.

There are several potential sources of reference samples: (1) Personal items used by the victim (e.g., toothbrush, hairbrush, razor) and banked samples from the victim (e.g., banked sperm or archival biopsy tissues stored in a medical facility); (2) biological relatives of the victim (i.e., "blood kin"); and (3) human remains previously identified through other modalities or other fragmented remains already typed by DNA. Often, there are severe limitations with remains or reference samples. For example, environmentally harsh conditions at the incident site may limit the quantity of DNA recoverable from human remains. There may be a paucity of personal items. For example, airline passengers often travel with their toothbrushes and hairbrushes, and these items may be lost or destroyed in an airline disaster. Kinship samples may be unavailable or scarce because the victim had few living biological relatives or because the relatives are unable or choose not to participate in the identification effort. In the case of airline disasters, families often travel together, further limiting the availability of known kinship samples. Finally, public perception and expectation may play a role in deciding whether DNA testing will be used to make identifications. All these factors must be considered when assessing the usefulness of DNA analysis for a particular incident.[6]

CHAPTER 7

Firearms

Firearms examination is one of the key services a forensic science laboratory provides; even smaller laboratories with only a few employees will probably have a firearms examiner. Many crimes are committed with a firearm, to coerce cooperation or directly harm, and society has judged this implied or actual violence to be a severe crime. Firearms examination is complex, technical, and detailed; it is experiencing a renaissance with the development and growth of automated database searches. This computerization promises to revolutionize the nature of firearms examination and, perhaps, forensic science.

In 1863, Confederate General Stonewall Jackson was fatally wounded on the battlefield in the U.S. Civil War. The deadly projectile was excised from his body and, through examination of its size and shape, determined to be .67-caliber ball ammunition. This was not the .58-caliber *minie* ball used by the Union army but ammunition typical of the Confederate forces—Jackson had been shot by one of his own soldiers! In 1876, a Georgia state court allowed the testimony of an expert witness on the topic of firearms analysis. These are the first examples of firearms analysis and testimony in the United States.

The field of forensic firearms examination is sometimes referred to as "ballistics" or "forensic ballistics." This terminology is not wholly accurate: Ballistics is the study of an object in flight and is under the domain of physics. The phrase "Forensic ballistics" may be somewhat more accurate but does not capture what forensic firearms examiners do in their job. They certainly are not analyzing the trajectories of bullets *while* the bullets are in flight! Many of the principles, equations, and methodology of ballistics are used, for example, to reconstruct a shooting incident. But the discipline of forensic firearms science is more than that; it encompasses the study of firearms, their manufacture, operation, and performance, the analysis of ammunition and its by-products (such as muzzle-to-target distance and gunshot residue), and the individualizing characteristics that are transferred from firearms to bullets and cartridge cases.

Types of Firearms

Very generally, firearms can be divided into two types: Handguns and shoulder firearms. Handguns include revolvers and pistols while shoulder firearms are more diverse, encompassing rifles, shotguns, machine guns, and submachine guns. A broad knowledge and familiarity with the various types, makes, models, and styles of firearms is crucial to being a successful forensic firearms scientist. This knowledge and familiarity should not only cover new products as they emerge on the market but also older models and the history of manufacturers and their products.

Handguns are firearms designed to be fired with one hand. These appear in two major types, revolvers and (semi)automatic pistols. A revolver is a handgun that feeds ammunition into the firing chamber by means of a revolving cylinder. The cylinder can swing out to the side or be hinged to the frame and released by a latch or a pin for loading and unloading. A single-action revolver requires that the hammer be cocked each time it is fired; a double-action revolver can be cocked by hand or by the pulling of the trigger which also rotates the cylinder.

A (semi)automatic pistol, on the other hand, feeds ammunition by means of a spring-loaded vertical magazine. Although the term "automatic" is often applied to pistols fed by magazines, they are not truly automatic in their firing. An automatic firearm is one that continues to fire ammunition while the trigger is depressed; a semiautomatic firearm fires one bullet for each pull of the trigger. When fired, semiautomatic pistols use the energy of the recoil and the sliding of the breech block (slide) or the recoil of the cartridge to expel the empty cartridge from the firearm and load a live round into the firing chamber. Springs are used to store the energy and expend it.

Shoulder arms consist of rifles, automatic rifles, machine guns, and shotguns. Rifles are designed to be fired from the shoulder with two hands. Rifles may be single-shot, repeating, semiautomatic or automatic. A single-shot rifle must be loaded and fired; the cartridge must be extracted, and then reloaded. Just after the turn of the century it was common as a young boy's first firearm, but it is almost nonexistent now. Repeating rifles fire one bullet with each pull of the trigger, but the expended cartridge must be expelled, cocked, and reloaded from a magazine manually. Repeating rifles may be bolt-action (like the M1 from war movies or many hunting rifles) or lever-action (made popular by cowboy movies). Semiautomatic rifles use the energy of the fired ammunition to expel the empty cartridge, cock the firing mechanism, and reload a live round; thus one pull of the trigger fires one round and this may be done sequentially until the magazine is empty. Assault rifles, like the AK-47 or M-16, can be fired either like semiautomatic rifles or in automatic mode: Pull the trigger and the firearm will fire ammunition continuously until all the ammunition is gone. A machine gun is a fully automatic firearm and therefore is fed ammunition from a high-capacity belt or box. Because of their size and the strength of the recoil, machine guns are meant to be fired from a tripod or other mounted/fixed positions. A submachine gun is a machine gun meant to be fired while held in the hands.

Firearm Barrels

The interior surface of the barrels of the firearms discussed so far (handguns and rifles, but not shotguns) is rifled with a series of ridges and valleys, called lands and grooves, respectively, which spiral the length of barrel. The lands dig into the bullet surface as these travel down the barrel, imparting spin to stabilize the bullet's flight once it leaves the barrel. This creates land and groove impressions on the bullet surface as well as impressions of the microscopic imperfections of the interior barrel surface called striations or striae.

During manufacture of a barrel, a hole is drilled down the length of a steel bar of the proper size for the intended firearm. The grooves are cut into the barrel by either a large segmented tool, called a broach, or a rifling button, a stiff metal rod with a flanged tip, which is run down the length of the hole. The grooves are cut in a spiral of a certain direction or twist (right-handed/clockwise or left-handed/counterclockwise); this spins the bullet and creates a stable flight path. Some manufacturers produce barrels with four grooves, some with five or six, depending on the design and desired performance of the firearm.

The interior or bore diameter of a rifled barrel is the diameter of a circle that touches the tops of the lands. The caliber of a firearm used to mean the same thing as bore diameter but now it refers mostly to the size of a particular ammunition cartridge; firearms are still referred to by their nominal caliber, however. A barrel's internal diameter is an exact measurement while caliber is an approximation; the barrel of a .38-firearm may actually measure between 0.345 and 0.365 in. (also note that calibers do not use the zero before the decimal). The caliber of American and British ammunition is typically measured in inches and all others are measured in millimeters (a Smith and Wesson .32 vs. a Beretta 9 mm).

Shotguns can fire numerous projectiles, called pellets or "shot" of varying sizes; they may also fire single projectiles called slugs. A single-barrel shotgun can be either single-shot (manually loaded) or repeating-shot in design (with a spring-loaded autofeeder or manual pump feeder with a reservoir of 3–5 shells). The interior of a shotgun barrel is smooth so that nothing deflects or slows down the pellets as they traverse its length. The muzzle of a shotgun barrel may be constricted by the manufacturer to produce a choke which helps to keep the pellets grouped long after they leave the barrel. The influence of choke on the shot pattern increases with the distance the pellets travel; the range of a shotgun is, compared with that of rifles, short but the choke can improve the chance of hitting targets at near-to-mid ranges. The choke may also be modified by barrel inserts.

The diameter of the shotgun barrel is called gauge and is the number of lead balls with the same diameter as the barrel that would weigh one pound. For example, 12 lead balls, which together weigh one pound, have the same diameter as the interior of a 12-gauge shotgun (about 0.729 in.). The exception to this system is the so-called 410-guage shotgun, which has its bore diameter measured in inches (0.410 in.).

Anatomy of Ammunition

Ammunition is what a firearm fires; it is typically a self-contained cartridge that comprises one or more projectiles, propellant (to act as fuel), and a primer (to ignite the propellant). As with firearms, ammunition comes in two major types: Bullets, for handguns and rifles, and shells, for shotguns.

Bullets, the first type of projectile, can be classified as lead (or lead alloy), fully jacketed, and semijacketed. Lead (alloy) bullets are a piece of lead hardened with minute amounts of other metals (such as antimony) and formed into the desired shape. Although hardened, they are too soft to use in most modern firearms other than .22-rifles or pistols. A fully jacketed bullet has a lead core which is encased in a harder material, usually copper-nickel alloys or steel. A semijacketed bullet has a metal jacket that covers only a portion of the bullet with the nose often exposed.

Because the nose of the bullet is softer than the surrounding jacket, the tip expands or "mushrooms" on impact, transferring its energy to the target. A hollow-point bullet is a semijacketed bullet that has a hollowed-out tip to increase this effect. Some semijacketed bullets leave the base exposed but cover the tip; these have a greater penetrating power due to the hardness of the tip material and tend to pass through the target.

Shotguns, as noted above, can fire pellets or slugs. Dozens of varieties of projectiles, from explosive bullets to "safety" ammunition consisting of pellets in a small sack to disable airline hijackers, are currently available and may be encountered in casework.

The propellant is the fuel that propels the projectile down and out of the firearms' barrel. By far the most common by far propellant, smokeless powder, was developed in response to the huge plumes of smoke that black powder produces on ignition. Smokeless powder is composed of cellulose nitrate combined with various chemicals to stabilize the mix and modify it for safe manufacture and transport.

The primer ignites the propellant. It consists of a small metal cup containing a percussion-sensitive material (it explodes on impact) that, when struck, creates enough heat to ignite the propellant. The small cup is set at the rear of the cartridge where it is struck by the firing pin. Modern primer materials consist of lead styphnate, antimony sulfide, barium nitrate, and tetracene. Because of the concerns of toxicity over long-term exposure to law enforcement officers, many primers are now made from organic primers that are lead-free.

What Happens When Ammunition Is Discharged?

When the hammer strikes the primer cap on a live round chambered in a weapon, the primer explodes and ignites the propellant. The burning of the propellant generates hot gases which expand and push the bullet from its cartridge case and down the barrel. The propellant is designed and the ammunition constructed so as to continue to burn—if the propellant stopped burning, the friction between the bullet and the rifling of the barrel would cause the bullet to stop. The friction between the bullet and the rifling also transfers the pattern of lands and grooves to the bullet's exterior. More importantly, it also transfers the microscopic striations—themselves transferred to the barrel's inner surface from the tool used to cut the lands and grooves—and these are used by the forensic firearms scientist in the microscopical comparison of known and questioned bullets.

If the firearm retains the spent cartridge, a revolver, for example, the only marks to be found on the cartridge that could be used for comparison would be the firing pin impression, the mark made by the firing pin as it strikes the primer cap. Firearms that expel the spent cartridge, however, may produce a variety of marks indicative of the method of cartridge extraction (extraction marks) and ejection (ejection marks) from the chamber. Another kind of common mark left on a cartridge case during discharge is called breech marks. The discharge of a firearm creates recoil, forcing the cartridge case backward into the breech face of the firearm; the breech face holds the base of the cartridge case in the chamber. Recoil causes the cartridge base to smack against the breech face and receive an impression of any imperfections in the breech face.

As the bullet leaves the muzzle of the barrel, it is followed by a plume of the hot gases that forced it down the barrel. This plume contains a variety of materials, such as partially burned gunpowder flakes, microscopic molten blobs of the primer chemicals, the bullet, and the cartridge. As these materials strike, or come to rest on, a surface, they transfer potential evidence of that surface's distance from the firearm's muzzle and other materials that may indicate that surface's association with the firing of a firearm or one that has been fired.

Bullet Comparisons

Many published studies have demonstrated that no two firearms produce the same unique marks on fired bullets and cartridge cases—this is true even with firearms of the same make and model. The machining of the manufacturing process, combined with the use of the firearm, leaves surface marks on the metal parts of the firearm that are not reproducible in other firearms. These marks are transferred to the bullets and casings when discharged from the firearm.

Because there is no practical method of comparing the striations on the inner surface of a rifled weapon with the striations on a fired bullet, reference bullets of the same make, style, and caliber must be used, and striations created by firing them from the questioned firearm. Not only would cutting the barrel open be impractical, but also the comparison would then be between positive (the barrel) and negative (the questioned bullet) impressions. The known fired bullets must be captured and preserved, however, so that they are as "pristine" as possible and not deformed or damaged. Firearms are typically discharged into a water tank where the water slows and eventually stops the bullet without altering its striations; other bullet recovery systems are used from the simple (a bucket filled with rubber shavings) to the high tech (sandwiched layers of specialized materials) The known bullet is then recovered, labeled, and used as a reference in the comparison; multiple known bullets may be created, if necessary.

The questioned and known bullets are first examined with the naked eye and then with slight magnification. The number of lands, grooves, their twist, and the bullets' weights are recorded. Because these are higher order class characteristics, any deviations from the known bullet indicate that the two bullets were fired from different barrels. If the lands, grooves, and direction of twist all concur, the next step is microscopical comparison of the striations on the bullets.

The comparison is performed on a comparison stereomicroscope with special stages that facilitate positioning the bullets in the focal plane and allow for rotation of the bullets on their long axis. The bullets are positioned on the stages, one on each, both pointing in the same direction, and held in position with clay or putty; this allows for easy repositioning and the soft material will not mark the bullets' surfaces. The known bullet is then positioned to visualize a land or groove with distinctive striations. The questioned bullet is then rotated until a land or groove, comes into view with the same striation markings. The lands and grooves of the two bullets must have the same widths. More importantly, the two bullets must, in addition to being similar, have the same striation patterns with no significant differences. This last point is critical: Not only must the forensic firearms scientist see the positive correlation between the significant information on the bullets' surfaces, but he or she must also not see any unexplained differences. Each rifled barrel is unique: No two will have identical striation patterns. This is true even of barrels that have been rifled in succession, one after the other. It takes education, training, and mentoring to train a person's eye and judgment on the subtleties of bullet striation patterns.

Firearm Databases and Automated Search Systems

Whether a firearm is used by the same criminal or shared between members of a criminal enterprise, firearm evidence can link a person or persons to multiple crimes. The problem in doing so is the difficulty of searching and comparing numerous bullets or casings. If the crimes were committed across multiple jurisdictions, the task becomes even more complex.

Two automated search systems were developed in the 1990s, one by the Federal Bureau of Investigation, called DRUGFIRE, which analyzed cartridge casing markings, and the other by the Bureau of Alcohol, Tobacco, and Firearms, called the Integrated Ballistic Identification System (IBIS), which primarily analyzed bullet striations but could also work with cartridge casings. The systems integrated digital imaging, novel data collection, computerized data bases of images, and communications technology. Unfortunately, the systems were not compatible with each other and specialized hardware and software was needed for each.

In January 1996, the ATF and the FBI acknowledged the need for IBIS and DRUGFIRE to be compatible. This meant the systems had to capture an image according to a standard protocol and with a minimum quality standard and exchange these images electronically so that an image captured on one system could be analyzed on the other. In June 1996, the National Institute of Standards and Technology (NIST) issued the minimal specifications for this data exchange. In May 1997, the National Integrated Ballistics Information Network (NIBIN) was born.

By 2002, the NIBIN program had expanded to 222 sites. When completed in all 16 multistate regions, NIBIN will be available at approximately 235 sites, covering every state and major population center. Since the inception of this technology, over 5,300 "hits" have been logged, providing investigative leads in many cases where none would otherwise have existed.

CHAPTER **8**

Anthropology

Anthropology is the study of humans, their cultures, and their biology. Anthropology can be divided into the study of human biology and human culture; and these can be further divided into the study of the past and the study of the present. This presents us with four main disciplines within anthropology:

Paleoanthropology	The *biological* study of *past* human populations
Bioanthropology	The *biological* study of *current* human populations
Archaeology	The study of *past* human *cultures*
Ethnology	The study of *current* human *cultures*

Forensic anthropology is the application of the study of humans to situations of modern legal or public concern. This typically takes the form of collecting and analyzing human skeletal remains to help identify victims and reconstruct the events surrounding their deaths. Why would not a medical doctor or pathologist perform these analyses? As medical doctors, pathologists learn about the body's various organ systems; additionally, forensic pathologists learn what makes these systems stop working. Forensic anthropologists are taught about only one system in the body: The skeleton. They learn to identify minute pieces of bone, recognizing hints that might indicate what portion of what bone they are holding. Pathologists require assistance from the advanced, focused knowledge of skeletal anatomy that anthropologists have just as anthropologists require assistance from the detailed and extensive medical training that pathologists gain in medical school. Pathologists generally do not learn about the bits and pieces that are the clues forensic anthropologists use to identify human remains.

Forensic anthropology involves methods from all of the anthropological disciplines but mostly from paleoanthropology and bioanthropology because of the study of the human skeleton. Archaeological methods are employed to collect the remains and paleoanthropological techniques are used to identify and analyze the bones to determine sex, age, race, and other biological descriptors. Forensic anthropology is therefore multidisciplinary in nature and requires a professional with the proper education, training, and experience to assist investigators.

The Human Skeleton

The human skeleton consists of 206 bones, most of which are paired (left and right) or grouped by area (e.g., the skull or the spine). Bone may seem like a "dead" material because it is so hard and inflexible. In reality, the skeleton is a very active organ system that can repair itself and alter its form over time. Bone, as a tissue and a structure, responds to the stresses placed on it, adding or subtracting bony material as needed. This activity that takes place throughout our lives, in addition to the genetic potential we inherit from our parents, results in the biological and anatomical variation we see between and within populations and individuals.

Bones perform four main functions for the body: Support, motion, protection, and growth. First, the skeleton provides the infrastructure for attachment and support of the softer tissues in our bodies. Second, these attachments allow the bones to act as levers, providing motion, powered by muscles, at the joints. The structure and arrangement of our bones set the range of motion for our limbs and bodies. Third, the hard bones protect our soft organs from physical damage; this is especially true of the brain (encased by the skull) and the heart and lungs (enclosed within the spine and rib cage). Fourth and finally, the bones are centers of growth from infancy through to early adulthood; they also continue to perform important physiological functions throughout our lives by housing the tissue that makes red blood cells. Bones supply us with a ready source of calcium if our dietary intake of that mineral is too low for too long.

Bone Organization and Growth

Bone growth and maintenance are complex processes that continue throughout our lives. Our skeletons must grow, mature, and repair at the macro- and microscopic levels even as we use them. An understanding of how bones grow and are organized is central to many of the analyses that forensic anthropologists perform. Two types of bone growth characterize the human skeleton: Endochondral and intramembranous. *Endochondral* bone growth starts with a "model" of a bone consisting of cartilage and *centers of ossification*. Bone is produced from these centers and it infiltrates the cartilage model which itself continues to grow. The developing shaft of the bone is called the *diaphysis* and the ends are called *epiphyses*. The growing areas eventually meet and the bone knits together. Not all epiphyses unite at the same time and the sequence of union is important for estimating age at death for individuals younger than about 20 years. In *intramembranous* bone growth, instead of a cartilage model, the ossification occurs within a membrane and this occurs in many bones of the skull. Bone differs from cartilage by having its collagenous connective tissue matrix impregnated with inorganic salts (primarily calcium phosphate and lesser amounts of calcium carbonate, calcium fluoride, magnesium phosphate, and sodium chloride). The osteoblasts, which form the osseous tissue, become encapsulated in lacunae but maintain contact with the vascular system via microscopic canaliculi. When they become encapsulated, they are referred to as osteocytes.

A characteristic feature of a cross-section of the shaft (diaphysis) of a long bone is its organization in concentric rings around a central canal containing a blood vessel. This is called a Haversian system (osteon). Between neighboring Haversian systems are nonconcentric lamellae, devoid of Haversian canals, termed interstitial lamellae. Vascular canals, called Volkmann's canals, traverse the long axis of the bone; they are always at right angles to Haversian canals. Their function is to link vascular canals of adjacent Haversian systems with each other and with the periosteal and endosteal blood vessels of the bone. The outer perimeter of a long bone, beneath the osteogenic connective tissue (called periosteum), is composed of circumferential lamellae, which also lack Haversian canals. This thick-walled hollow shaft of compact bone (the diaphysis) contains bone marrow. At the distal ends of long bones, where Haversian systems are not found, the bone appears spongy and is therefore called cancellous, or spongy, bone. The spongy appearance is misleading, because careful examination of the architecture reveals a highly organized trabecular system providing maximal structural support with minimal density of bony tissue.

The epiphyses at the ends of the diaphysis or shaft contain the spongy bone covered by a thin layer of compact bone. The cavities of the epiphyseal spongy bone are in contact with the bone marrow core of the diaphysis except during growth of long bones in young animals. Interposed between the epiphysis and the diaphysis is the cartilaginous epiphyseal plate. The epiphyseal plate is joined to the diaphysis by columns of cancellous bone; this region is known as the metaphysis.

When bone is formed and replaces a cartilaginous "model," the process is termed endochondral ossification. Some parts of the skull develop from osteogenic mesenchymal connective tissue, however, without a cartilaginous "model" having been formed first. This is termed intramembranous ossification, and these bones are called membrane bones. In both instances, three types of cells are associated with bone formation, growth, and maintenance: osteoblasts, osteocytes, and osteoclasts. The osteoblasts produce osseous tissue (bone), become embedded in the matrix they manufacture, and are then renamed osteocytes, to reflect their change of status. They remain viable, because they have access to the vascular supply via microscopic canaliculi through which cellular processes extend to receive nutrients and oxygen. Osteoclasts actively resorb and remodel bone as required for growth; these are giant, multinuclear, phagocytic, and osteolytic cells.

Bones consist of an outer layer of hard, smooth compact bone, also called cortical bone. The inner layer is an infrastructure of spongelike bone called trabecullar bone in long bones, which increases the structural strength of the bone without additional weight. In the very center of long bones is the medullary cavity which contains marrow, a fatty material that also houses blood-generating tissues. In life, this composite architecture creates a very strong but resilient framework for our bodies.

The microstructure of bone is quite complex and organized. Specialized growth cells (osteoblasts) produce bone and deposit it in layers, eventually becoming encapsulated in a self-made chamber (lacuna; plural lacunae). They maintain contact with the circulatory system and other bone cells through microscopic vascular channels through which cellular processes extend to receive nutrients and oxygen. When an osteoblast becomes fully encapsulated, it is referred to as an osteon.

The third main type of bone cell, osteoclasts, actively break down and remodel bone as required for growth. When an osteocyte reaches the end of its productivity, it dies and the bone around is reworked and made available to new osteoblasts. In response to the stresses our activities place on our skeletons, the interaction between osteoblasts, osteocytes, and osteoclasts model and shape our bones. Because new osteons are formed by remodeling existing structures, bone has a patchwork appearance at the cellular level. Bone that lies between recently reworked bone is called interstitial bone; the amounts of new, reworked, and old bone is an indication of how old someone is and we will see later how this can provide an estimate of age at death.

Skeletal Anatomy

Before describing the human skeletal anatomy, it is important to discuss the proper handling of human remains. Most people encounter skeletons only on Halloween or at a costume party. Given that they are potent symbols of death (which is what they represent in those contexts), it is only natural that people feel nervous or anxious when presented with the real thing. The urge to gesture, joke around, or taunt others with a bone or skull is simply a way of expressing that unease, by laughing at "the Grim Reaper." What you must keep in mind, however, is that the material you are handling was once part of a human being, like yourself, with a life, family, feelings, and dignity. Additionally, every specimen is unique and irreplaceable, so it must be handled with care. Bones should always be held over a table, preferably with a padded or protected surface. The skull is of special consideration due to its delicacy and centrality to a forensic examination. The bones of the nose and the eye orbits, and the teeth, are fragile. The skull should be handled by the sides and base in both hands with a firm grasp.

The cranial skeleton refers only to the skull; everything else is called the postcranial skeleton (meaning below the cranial skeleton). The axial skeleton describes the spine (vertebrae), ribs, and breastbone (sternum). The grouping of either upper limb bones (including the shoulder) or lower limb bones (excluding the pelvis) is called the appendicular skeleton.

Collecting Human Remains

Forensic anthropologists rarely find skeletal remains that are above ground. It is often a hiker, hunter, or some other civilian in a remote or uninhabited area who stumbles across the bones at a crime scene. Because the "evidence" has been found by untrained persons, securing the scene is the most effective way of initiating evidence protection. The subsequent searching of an area for bones is similar to processing other crime scenes, however, and proceeds as an orderly, careful search by trained personnel. This search may be aided by various detection methods, such as probes that detect the gases produced by decomposition, radar that penetrates into the ground, or even the so-called cadaver dogs trained to sniff for the smells of human decomposition.

If the remains are scattered, each bone fragment should be flagged or marked. This provides a view of the pattern of dispersal and clues to the possible location the missing bones might lie. Context is even more important with skeletal remains and the individual bones should not be disturbed until the entire scene has been photographed and documented. All the bones on the surface, even animal bones, should be collected.

It requires more skill to retrieve buried remains. Archaeological techniques are employed to excavate buried skeletal materials and should be performed only by trained personnel under the supervision of an experienced archaeological excavator. A grid is set up with one point set as a datum, or reference point, from which all measurements originate. Each unit in the grid is excavated separately; the units may be processed at the same time or done in series. Soil and materials are removed a thin layer at a time (usually 2–5 cm) slowly exposing the buried items. Only after the bones have all been found, excavated, photographed, and documented will they be removed and transported for analysis.

Sometimes, humans, animals, and nature are not kind to skeletal remains. A skull or bone may not be whole when recovered and it must be reconstructed prior to analysis. Thin wooden sticks and glue usually do the trick, although other means may need to be used depending on how damaged the bone is. Subsequent analyses need to be kept in mind (carbon 14 dating, DNA, x-rays, etc.) to minimize any obstacles to their successful completion.

Analysis of Skeletal Materials

The first question the anthropologist must ask is, "Is the submitted material really bone?" With whole bones, this is obvious. A surprising number of materials can superficially resemble a bone fragment and even professionals need to be careful, especially with very small fragments. It may be necessary to take a thin section of the material and examine it microscopically for cell morphology. Elemental analysis is also very useful for small fragments, as few materials have the same elemental ratios as bone.

Once the material is determined to be bone, the second question is whether the bone is animal or human. This can present a greater challenge than it may appear at first. Pig bones, bear paws, and some sheep bones can, at first, appear similar to human bones. A comprehensive knowledge of human anatomy and a solid grounding in animal osteology will answer most of these questions. A comparative collection of cataloged skeletal remains is crucial to an accurate taxonomical assessment: It can be as useful to know what something is, as what it is not. Dr. Douglas Ubelaker writes of the following example in his book, *Bones*.[1] A bone fragment had been found in a remote part of Alaska. The bone displayed a fracture that had been repaired surgically with a metal plate. The extensive bone growth over the surgical plate indicated the patient had received the surgery long before death. Given the nature of the surgery and the surgical efforts, the authorities began to search for the surgeon who had performed the operation. After these efforts failed, the bone was sent to Dr. Ubelaker at the Smithsonian Institution, where a microscopic section revealed the bone to have a nonhuman bone cell morphology, one that closely matched that of a large dog. This explains why the surgeon could not be found—because the doctor was a veterinarian! This is an excellent example of why you should not make assumptions and not to come to a conclusion until you have all the facts.

The Biological Profile

Once the remains are determined to be human, a biological profile can be developed for the individual(s) represented. The biological profile consists of the sex, age at death, racial affinity, height, and any other aspects that would describe the individual class level information. The biological profile is the first step toward identifying whom the remains represent. It is a waste of time to immediately start comparing the dental x-rays or sequencing DNA samples of a 20-year-old woman when the bones recovered are from a 50-year-old man. The bones are present and their quality will determine what methods can be applied and, in part, the accuracy of those methods.

The criteria that help determine the biological profile are either qualitative, that is, morphological (the presence or absence of a trait, or the shape or size of a landmark) or quantitative. Physical anthropologists use many different measurements to discriminate between individuals, samples, and populations. Some of this information has been cataloged (for example, at the University of Tennessee's Forensic Data Bank) and used to provide virtual "comparative collections" of measurements that can be used by anyone with a computer (FORDISC is an example of commercially available software for forensic anthropologists). As more museums and universities surrender their osteological collections for repatriation and reburial, collections of data instead of bones will become increasingly crucial to future anthropologists' research. Quantitative physical anthropology is dominated by statistical analysis and sometimes analyses, such as principal component analysis, are quite complex involving many measurements, samples, and relationships.

Male or Female?

Although in life the differences between males and females are almost always obvious, these differences are not always so apparent, especially when the visual cues the flesh provides are gone. Males can be up to 20% larger than females but in some instances there is little or no difference in size. Many of the quantitative skeletal traits overlap in the middle of the distribution of their values and statistical analysis is required to sort out equivocal examples.

Sexual differences in the human skeleton begin before birth although they are not truly diagnostic until after puberty. In general, females' postcranial skeleton develops faster than males and this difference in rate can be used to infer sex in prepubertal individuals. Typically, however, sex should not be estimated unless the individual is of an age where puberty has begun; above 18 years of age, sex can be determined with confidence.

The significant differences between males and females are size and function-related morphology. The two areas that are used most often to determine the sex of an individual in life are also the most diagnostic in death: The pelvis and the skull. Other bones can be very useful for estimating sex as well, and with only a few measurements an experienced forensic anthropologist can be accurate 70%–90% of the time.

The largest number of and most accurate traits for determining sex reside in the pelvis. The major reason that male and female skeletal anatomy differs so much in the pelvic region is that only females carry and bear babies; human pelvic anatomy reflects this functional difference. Thus, the male pelvis tends to be larger and more robust while the female pelvis is broader and can exhibit pregnancy-specific traits. A useful trait for distinguishing between the male and female pelvis is the sciatic notch, located on the inferior lateral border of the ilium. The sciatic notch is wide (an angle of about 60 degrees) in females and narrow in males (about 30 degrees).

A very reliable method for determining the sex from pelvis is the Phenice method, developed by Dr. Terrell Phenice in 1969, which uses three characteristics: The ventral arc, the subpubic concavity, and the ischio-pubic ramus. The ventral arc is a ridge on the anterior surface of the pubic bone that is present in females but absent in males. The subpubic concavity is a depression on the medial border of the ischio-pubic ramus, just inferior to the pubic symphysis. The concavity is wider and deeper in females and is only slight, if at all present, in males. Finally, the ischio-pubic ramus itself is flatter and thinner in males whereas in females it is wide and may even have a ridge on it. It is possible to be accurate in sexing a pelvis with only these three traits. One cannot rely on the Phenice method alone, however, as the pelvic remains may be fragmentary and the pubic bone may be absent. Numerous measurements have been used along with statistical analysis to derive more objective sexing methods than descriptive anatomy. Often, these methods are as accurate as morphological traits but they are important for gauging slight differences between anatomically similar populations.

Sex can be estimated from the cranium as well as the pelvis but the traits may not always be as obvious. Males tend to be larger and have larger muscle attachments than females. The specific areas of interest are the brow ridges, mastoid processes (bony masses just behind the ears for attachment of neck muscles), occipital area at the rear of the skull, upper palate, and the general architecture of the skull.

The skull is one of the most, if not the most, studied, measured, and examined part of the skeleton. This enthusiasm for measurement extends to the determination of sex. Thirty-four standard measurements are the minimum for inclusion of a skull into the National Forensic Data Base, and from these sex can be estimated. These measurements are taken with specialized rulers, called calipers that are either spreading calipers or sliding calipers. The measurements are taken from various landmarks around the skull. Complicated statistical techniques are used to sort out the measurements, relate them to each other, and then compare them against an appropriate reference population. Software developed at the University of Tennessee, called FORDISC, provides an easy way to analyze and compare data from skeletons.

Postcranial bones can also provide information about a person's sex, but most of these are based on size and therefore are quantitative. Many of the postcranial bone measurements will yield an accuracy of between 58–100%. The measurement may be straightforward but the interpretation may not be. For example, if the head of the femur is greater than 48 mm, the person would most likely be male; a measurement of less than 43 mm indicates a female. A measurement of 43–48 mm indicates that the size of the person was such that estimating sex from this measurement alone would give an inconclusive result. This is why it is very important to consider all the recovered bones before making a judgment and, in turn, this emphasizes the need for a comprehensive search and collection of the remains at the scene.

Age at Death

As we develop in the womb, grow into adults, and age over the years, our skeletons change in known and predictable ways. For infants and children, this is the appearance and development of skeletal growth areas that spread, meet, and fuse into whole bones. As adults, our skeleton's growth shifts to maintenance functions, responding to new stresses, such as exercise (or lack of it) and job-related activities. Our later years bring with them the loss of bone mass, the slowing of our physiology, and the general degradation that accompanies our senior years. These changes are all recorded in our skeletons and forensic anthropologists use these alterations to estimate a person's age at death.

Estimating age is conceptually different from estimating sex: there are only two sexes but age is a continuum of 70, 80, or 90 (sometimes more) years. The age-related changes in our skeletons are predictable but not specific enough to allow for an estimate of "31 years and 8 months." The natural variation within a population and between individuals in a population prohibits a precise determination of age. Estimated age ranges, bracketed around the most likely age (e.g., 25–35 years) are the most acceptable way of reporting age at death. This bracketing necessarily leads to imprecision because accuracy is retained only up to a point. If you always estimate that an individual's age is between 1 and 95 years, you will almost always be correct. That estimate, however, would not be very useful to investigators. By balancing the natural variation in aging and the anthropologist's skill with the methods used, an estimate that accurately reflects the precision of the sample *and* technique can be produced.

For the sake of convenience and organization, the range of human age has been broken into various classes with associated years: fetal (before birth), infant (0–3), child (3–12), adolescent (12–20), young adult (20–35), adult (35–50), and old adult (50+). These represent the significant phases of growth, maturation, and decline in the skeleton and related tissues.

Bones can indicate the stage of development attained by the appearance and fusion of the various epiphyses throughout the body. Nonunited epiphyses are easy to observe because the diaphyseal surface is characteristically rough and irregular in appearance. Epiphyseal appearance and union occurs over the course of years and is a process, not an event; the degree of union (usually scored on a multipoint scale) must be carefully assessed as this could indicate which extreme of an age range is being observed. The three main stages of union are, first, the epiphysis is open; second, the epiphysis is united but the junction is still visible; and, third, the epiphysis is completely fused. Epiphyses can be small and every effort should be made during collection to make sure none are overlooked.

Although epiphyses all over the body are uniting from infancy onward, the major epiphyses of the bones of modern populations fuse between 13 and 18 years of age (see table 8.1). Union typically occurs in the order of elbow, hip, ankle, knee, wrist, and shoulder. Note that the beginning of epiphyseal union overlaps with the end of dental development and, therefore, these two methods complement one another. The last epiphysis to fuse is usually the medial clavicle (collarbone) in the early 20s. Once all of the epiphyses have fused, by about age 28 for most of the population, the growth of the skeleton stops and other age indicators must be used.

Table 8.1 Ages of union for long bones

Bone	Epiphysis	Female Ages	Male Ages
Innominate	Ilium-pubis	7–9	7–9
Humerus	Lateral epicondyle	10–14	11–17
Humerus	Medial epicondyle	13–15	15–18
Fibula	Distal	13–16	14–18
Radius	Head (Proximal)	13–16	14–19
Femur	Head	13–17	15–18
Tibia	Distal	14–16	14–18
Femur	Distal	14–17	14–19
Tibia	Proximal	14–17	15–19
Fibula	Proximal	14–18	14–20
Humerus	Head	14–20	14–21
Radius	Distal	16–19	16–20
Ulna	Distal	16–19	18–20
Ulna	Proximal	13–15	14–15
Innominate	Iliac crest	17–19	17–20
Clavicle	Medial	17–21	18–22

A few areas of the skeleton continue to change in subtle ways (compared with the appearance and union of epiphyses) throughout the remainder of adulthood. The main areas used for estimating adult age are found on the pelvic bones, the ribs, and the continuous remodeling of bone's cellular structure. These few, relatively small areas of the human skeleton have been intensely studied and restudied over the years by researchers trying to fine-tune the estimation of age at death for adults. Any single method alone, however, runs the risk of misleading the investigator and all available information must be considered, including physical evidence which is not of an anthropological nature (clothing, personal effects, etc.).

The pubic symphysis (a symphysis is a "false" joint) is the junction of the two pubic bones lying roughly four to five inches below your navel. This junction is bridged by cartilage that acts as a cushion between the two bones. The symphyseal face is a raised platform that slowly changes over the years from a rough, rugged surface to a smooth, well-defined area. The morphological changes of the pubic symphysis are considered by the majority of anthropologists to be among the most reliable estimators of age at death. This area was first studied in depth by Todd, who divided the changes he saw into ten phases, each defined phase relating to an age range. Todd's work was later advanced by McKern and Stewart who broke Todd's holistic method into a sectional evaluation in order to simplify the process. McKern and Stewart's work was based on young males who were killed in the Korean War and this may have unintentionally biased their results; their work was, after all, focused on identifying soldiers of that very same sex/age category. Nevertheless, the McKern and Stewart method held sway for a number of years until Judy Suchey and Allison Brooks began a large-scale collection and analysis project on the pubic symphysis by collecting samples from the Los Angeles County morgue. The intention was to collect a wide-ranging demographically accurate sample that could be assessed not only for age but also for variations due to an individual's sex. Their results are more akin to Todd's than McKern and Stewart's, although with fewer phases of development.[2]

Another area of morphological change with advancing adulthood is the sternal end of the fourth left rib. As the cartilage between the sternum and the ribs ages, it begins to ossify at a known and predictable rate. Another method of estimating age at death is the examination of the changes in the auricular surface, where the ilium attaches to the sacrum (the so-called sacro-illiac joint). As age progresses, the surface of the bone becomes less bumpy and more smooth, with smallish pores opening up creating a decrease in the organization of the surface traits.

Finally, bone never rests. It is constantly remodeling in response to the stresses placed upon it. This remodeling can be seen in the microscopic structure of bone. In approximately the same way as a wall would be rebuilt, bone first needs to be torn down before it can be built up. This constant erosion and renewal leave permanent markers in bone: once we die, these changes cease. Therefore, a correlation exists between the amount of bone reworking and the amount of time the body has expended energy on this remodeling. A thin section of bone is cut, specific areas are viewed microscopically, and the various structural elements (whole osteons, fragmented osteons, interstitial bone fragments, etc.) are counted. Various formulae have been developed and are among the most accurate methods available for estimating age at death. A major disadvantage of this method is that some amount of bone must be removed which may or may not be allowed because of case requirements.

Ancestry

Many of the cues we use to assess someone's ancestry in life are not well demonstrated in the skeleton. Moreover, ancestry or "race" is a difficult concept, both biologically and socially: Human physical variation is often a subtle thing and people are sensitive to the labels other people place on them. While it is true that no pure ethnic groups exist (or have ever existed), we identify people based partly on what we perceive their "race" to be. This combination of blurred ancestral categories and popular perception, not to mention people's racial self-identity, make ancestry one of the most difficult estimations in a forensic anthropologist's examination. Nonetheless, forensic anthropologists are routinely called upon to assess skeletal remains for clues to that person's ancestral affiliation to help lead police toward identification. The terms forensic anthropologists use to designate ancestry are typically those of the U.S. Census, namely, Whites, Blacks, Hispanics, Asians, Native Americans, and Other (www. census.gov).

Ancestry can be estimated by morphological or quantitative analysis and both these methods are centered on the skull. Features of the skull, such as the general shape of the eye orbits, nasal aperture, dentition and surrounding bone, and the face can offer indications of ancestry. Other features, such as the scooped-out appearance of the lingual (tongue) side of the upper central incisors often found in individuals of Asian ancestry (so-called shovel-shaped incisors) are more distinct. But even indicators such as these are not as clear as they may appear at first glance: Prehistoric Native Americans migrated into North America across the Bering Strait from Asia and some of them show shovel-shaping on their incisors.

In the hope of rendering ancestral assessment more objective, physical anthropologists sought metric means of categorizing human populations. Currently, these consist of numerous measurements which are then placed in formulae derived from analysis of known populations. While fairly accurate, these formulae suffer from being based on historically small samples that are not necessarily representative of modern populations. These concerns aside, given a complete skull or cranium, ancestral affiliation can be assessed with enough accuracy to make them useful for forensic investigations.

Stature

Our living stature directly relates to the length of our long bones, especially those of our lower limbs. Calculating stature from long bone lengths is relatively simple and even partial bones can yield useful results. The only difficulty is that sex and ancestry must be known to correctly estimate height because humans vary within and between these categories.

For example, a White male with a femur length of 55.88 cm would be estimated to have been between 189 cm and 196 cm ((2.38 * 55.88) + 61.41, +/− 3.27, rounding up) tall during life, or about 6 ft 1 in. to 6 ft 3 in.

Odontology

The most common role of the forensic dentist is the identification of deceased individuals. Dental identification can be conducted through comparison of dental remains to either antemortem or postmortem records. The most frequently performed examination is comparing the dentition of a deceased person with those of a person represented by antemortem to determine if they are the same individual. The biological profile developed by the forensic anthropologist is very helpful in narrowing down the potential choices for selecting the antemortem records. If the antemortem records are available, any postmortem x-rays should replicate the view and angle in the antemortem x-rays. If antemortem records are not available, a postmortem record is created by the forensic dentist for possible future comparisons. The forensic dentist produces the

Table 8.2 Formulae for calculating stature

Category	Stature =
White Males	3.08 * Humerus +70.45 +/− 4.05
	3.78 * Radius + 79.01 +/− 4.32
	3.70 * Ulna + 74.05 +/− 4.32
	2.38 * Femur + 61.41 +/− 3.27
	2.52 * Tibia + 78.62 +/− 3.37
	2.68 * Fibula + 71.78 +/− 3.29
Black Males	3.26 * Humerus +62.10 +/− 4.43
	3.42 * Radius + 81.56 +/− 4.30
	3.26 * Ulna + 79.29 +/− 4.42
	2.11 * Femur + 70.35 +/− 3.94
	2.19 * Tibia + 86.02 +/− 3.78
	2.19 * Fibula + 85.65 +/− 4.08
Asian Males	2.68 * Humerus +83.19 +/− 4.25
	3.54 * Radius + 82.00 +/− 4.60
	3.48 * Ulna + 77.45 +/− 4.66
	2.15 * Femur + 72.75 +/− 3.80
	2.40 * Fibula + 80.56 +/− 3.24

postmortem record by careful charting and written descriptions of the dental structures and by taking radiographs.

Once the postmortem record is complete, a comparison between it and any antemortem records can be conducted. The comparison is methodical and systematic: Each tooth and structure is examined and compared. Filings, caps, and restorations play the largest role in the identification process. Other features play a role in those individuals with good dental hygiene and few restorations. Similarities as well as explainable and unexplainable discrepancies should be noted during the comparison process. Those differences that can be explained typically encompass dental restorations that occurred in the time elapsed between the antemortem and postmortem records. Think of a person who had a tooth pulled or a cavity filled, for example. If a discrepancy, such as a postmortem tooth that is not present on the antemortem record, is unexplainable, the odontologist will conclude that two different people are represented (an exclusion).

Dental anatomy

The anatomy of the mouth is important to forensic science for a number of reasons. First, the teeth are made of enamel, the hardest substance that the body produces, and teeth can survive severe conditions and still be viable for analysis. Second, the teeth are the only part of the skeletal anatomy that directly interacts with the environment and, therefore, can reflect conditions the person experienced during life. Finally, teeth and their related structures have the potential to be used in the identification of the deceased. Because of these reasons and the complexity of fillings, braces, and other dental work, forensic odontologists, that is dental health professionals, who apply their skills to legal investigations, are a specialty often relied upon in cases of unidentified bodies, mass disasters, and missing person cases.

Forensic odontologists use a variety of methods to organize teeth and uniquely name each tooth in the mouth. The common names of teeth are also useful but they refer to a group of teeth with the same characteristics. Typically, a numbering method is used and one of the most common is to number the teeth from the lower right molar, moving anteriorly, to the lower left molar; the next tooth would then be the upper left molar and then back around to the upper right molar. This sections the mouth into four quadrants: Upper right, lower right, upper left, and lower left.

Each tooth has five sides: buccal, the side toward the cheek; lingual, the side toward the tongue; mesial, toward the midline of the body; distal, the side away from the midline; and the chewing surface called the occlusal surface. These orientations help to describe where a cavity or filling is located. Individually, each tooth has similar structures but is shaped differently according to its functions. Every tooth has a crown, body, and root.

Tooth development

Teeth grow from the chewing surface, or cusps, downward to the roots. This continual process is usually broken up into phases that relate to the amount of tooth development. Humans have two sets of teeth, one when we are children, called "baby" teeth but more properly termed "deciduous teeth," and the other when we are adults, called "permanent teeth." Dentists often have a dental development chart in their offices. Different teeth develop at different rates, with incisors developing faster than molars. Teeth erupt through the gums when they are about half to three quarters developed. Notable landmarks in tooth eruption are the first deciduous incisor at about nine months, the first permanent molar at about six years, the first permanent incisor at about seven years, and the third permanent molar at sometime between 15 and 21 years; the last tooth is notorious for irregular eruption and is not necessarily a reliable indicator of age.

Identification

The goal of a forensic is individualizing a set of human remains, often referred to as a "positive identification." This moves beyond class characteristics, no matter how narrow a classification is, into the realm of uniqueness. To achieve this level of certainty, the data have to support the conclusion that the remains represent those of one, and only one person to the exclusion of all other people.

Because most people regularly visit their dentists, dental records and x-rays are the most common form of antemortem record that leads to a positive identification. Because many years may have passed since the last x-ray and the forensic comparison, it may be necessary to have a skilled forensic odontologist consult on the examination. Any differences between the x-rays taken before death and after death must be explainable and not be significant for the identification to be positive.

Other x-rays can lead to positive identifications as well. A structure in the frontal bone, the frontal sinus, is considered to be unique to a reasonable degree of scientific certainty. Similarly, the internal structure of postcranial bones is considered to be unique as well. Surgeries, healed fractures, and disease may all be documented radiographically and also can lead to positive comparisons.

Identification through the comparison of ante- and postmortem x-rays is considered the best method for skeletal remains. People's teeth vary in size, number, and position and the amount, size, type, location, and extent of dental work also varies enormously from person to person. Taken in combination, this natural and medical variation is such that it would be unthinkable to find two people whose teeth *and* dental work were exactly the same. X-rays can also document other individualizing traits, such as the habitual wear mentioned earlier, and some of these may be corroborated by family or friends.

Cause versus Manner of Death

The cause of death is the action that initiates the cessation of life; the manner of death is the way in which this action came about. There are, literally, thousands of causes of death but there are only four manners in which to die: Natural, accidental, suicide, and homicide. Forensic anthropologists can sometimes assist a medical examiner with assessing the manner of death (e.g., see Sauer[3]) but only rarely can one assist with the cause of death. The fact that a skull exhibits an entrance and exit bullet hole, does not mean that is the cause of death; many people get shot every year, but only some of them die from their wounds. Similarly, a person may be strangled to death (cause: asphyxiation) but the strangulation may leave no markers on the skeleton. Forensic anthropologists must be very careful to stay within the bounds of their knowledge and training in order to provide the most useful information to medical examiners, investigators, and others who require their services.

Taphonomy

Taphonomy is the study of what happens to an organism from the time it dies until the time it ends up in the laboratory. In recent years, taphonomy has blossomed into a full-fledged area of study in its own right; this expansion has greatly assisted the various forensic sciences that relate directly to the study of the dead. This information greatly increases the ability of investigators to assess time since death, discern premortem (before death) from postmortem (after death) effects, and detect subtle clues that might help lead to a killer's identity or activity.

Pathology

Forensic anthropologists work closely with forensic pathologists and may often be able to provide information beyond what a pathologist may know. Certain aspects of the pathologist's and anthropologist's work necessarily overlap, however, and these most often are in the areas of wounding and healing of bone.

The distinction of greatest importance for forensic anthropologists is the differences between premortem and postmortem injuries. Living bone has different mechanical properties than dead, dried bone and this leads to different reactions to traumatic events. Any sign of healing in bone is definitive of a premortem injury. Wounds or breaks that occur near the time of death (called perimortem injuries) may be difficult to distinguish from trauma that occurs shortly after death because the body will not be alive long enough to begin noticeable healing. It is possible to distinguish between perimortem and long-term postmortem cuts by using electron microscopy: At the edge of a fresh cut, the soft tissue will have dried and pulled back from the edge of the cut, whereas in a bone cut after the soft tissue has dried it will be at the edge of the cut.

Forensic anthropology plays a central role in the identification of people who are not identifiable by fingerprints or photographs: Nature has taken its course. Using their knowledge of human anatomy and variation, forensic anthropologists develop biological profiles of skeletal remains and look for individualizing traits in the hope that the victim can be identified. They also assist other investigators, such as forensic odontologists and medical examiners, to help with the interpretation of taphonomic information and trauma.

CHAPTER 9

Expert Testimony

The culmination of a forensic scientist's efforts is a report on the examinations performed and then, if needed, testifying to those results in a court of law. Even if someone were the greatest scientist on earth but could not effectively testify to what they did, they would be a failure as a forensic scientist. A professional forensic scientist must be able to explain the theories, methods, procedures, analyses, results, and interpretations of the scientific examinations they performed. And they must do this without being an advocate for either side in a case: Impartiality is the hallmark of science and this is especially true of forensic science.

What Is the Difference between Civil and Criminal Cases?

Civil cases usually involve private disputes between persons or organizations. Criminal cases involve an action that is considered to be harmful to society as a whole.

Civil cases

A civil case begins when a person or entity (such as a corporation or the government), called the plaintiff, claims that another person or entity, called the defendant, has failed to carry out a legal duty owed to the plaintiff. Both the plaintiff and the defendant are referred to as parties or litigants. The plaintiff may ask the court to tell the defendant to fulfill the duty, or make compensation for the harm done, or both. Legal duties include respecting rights established under the constitution or under federal or state law.

Civil suits are brought in both state and federal courts. An example of a civil case in a state court would be if a citizen (including a corporation) sued another citizen for not living up to a contract. Individuals, corporations, and the federal government can also bring civil suits in a federal court claiming violations of federal statutes or constitutional rights. For example, the federal government can sue a hospital for overbilling Medicare and Medicaid, a violation of a federal statute. An individual can sue a local police department for violation of his or her constitutional rights—for example, the right to assemble peacefully.

Criminal case

A person accused of a crime is generally charged in a formal accusation called an indictment (for felonies or serious crimes) or information (for misdemeanors). The government, on behalf of the people of the United States, prosecutes the case through the United States Attorney's Office if the person is charged with a federal crime. A state's attorney's office prosecutes state crimes.

It is not the victim's responsibility to bring a criminal case. In a kidnapping case, for instance, the government would prosecute the kidnapper; the victim would not be a party to the action.

In some criminal cases, there may not be a specific victim. For example, state governments arrest and prosecute people accused of violating laws against driving while intoxicated because society regards that as a serious offense that can result in harm to others.

When a court determines that an individual committed a crime, that person will receive a sentence. The sentence may be an order to pay a monetary penalty (a fine and/or restitution to the victim), imprisonment, or supervision in the community (by a court employee called a U.S. probation officer if a federal crime), or a combination of any of these three things.

Writing Reports

Forensic science laboratory reports vary widely in their particular formats but all should contain the following information:

- The name of the examiner who conducted the tests
- The agency where the examiner works
- The date the report was issued

- The case identification information (laboratory number, case number, etc.)
- Contact information for the examiner
- The items examined
- The methods and instrumentation used to examine and analyze the submitted items
- The results of the examinations and/or analyses
- Any interpretations or statistics which are relevant to the results
- A statement of the disposition of the evidence
- The signatures of the examiner and any reviewers of the report (Many laboratories require that signatures be notarized)

The format of the report should roughly follow that of a standard scientific paper: Introduction, Materials and Methods, Results, Conclusions, and Discussion. It is important to remember, however, that, unlike a scientific paper in a peer-reviewed journal, a forensic science laboratory report is *not* intended for other scientists. Most of the readers of a forensic science laboratory report are law enforcement officers, attorneys, and judges all of whom may have little to no training in science. It requires a special effort to make the reports readable, intelligible, and concise while retaining the necessary information to maintain their scientific rigor. To this end, forensic science laboratory reports should be *summations* of analyses and not complete and definitive scientific research results.

Science is a public endeavor and articles are the canonical means of communicating original scientific results. By being published, they are meant for public scrutiny, both by the expert and the layperson. Scientific journal articles are formal communications from which one can legitimately infer the norms and values and the standards by which the scientific community operates.

Scientific text has several features that distinguish it from other types of text. The style is the syntax of sentences or the choice of words used to communicate the materials and methods, the results, and the discussion of the research. The presentation is the way the text is organized and the data are displayed. Finally, the argument is the means employed to support the claims made by the researchers.

Forensic laboratory reports differ from standard scientific articles published in journals in several important ways. These differences reflect the nature of forensic science and the requirements placed on its "science-ness" by the legal system.

Why are forensic reports not like scientific papers?

The seventeenth century scientific paper would be barely recognizable, as such, to us today, because the emphasis then was on the scientist, not the science. The text, devoid of technical vocabulary, was written in a first-person narrative. Its credibility was gained through the scientist's reliable testimony of what he observed and experienced with his own senses. Facts took precedence over argument but numerical data were conspicuous by their absence. Tables were the only means of expressing quantitative data. Plots or graphic presentations were not "invented" until late in the eighteenth century. Facts were bound by causation and not by theory; "A" caused "B" but not in any larger sense than that one-to-one relationship. Science was seen as a sort of museum, a storehouse of facts to be acquired, cataloged, and kept.

Twentieth-century scientific articles, by contrast, are heavy with technical vocabulary and focus on the relationships among sets of allied facts that are bound by theory. The structure of the article does not vary with the whims of its author; it has headings, sections, references, and so on. In fact, the abstract—the condensation of the article that appears at the beginning of a scientific article—was not "standardized" until about 1920. Quantification is now the major contributor to impression of an article's objectivity, not the testimonial of the author's senses. The style is impersonal, third-person, and free of adornments. Experiments are not the subject of the article in the twentieth century. They are a tool designed to produce results according to a theory. The argument is key—the data do not speak for themselves as in the seventeenth century—and interpretations can be derived from data only through the power of a sound argument.

Among the reasons for the change are:

- the increased complexity of science over the last few centuries
- the accumulation of knowledge
- higher standards of proof are demanded (personal experience is not enough)
- the greater volumes of data (standardized structure makes it easier to read, "skim," overview)

Forensic Science Reports

Forensic science reports as issued by laboratories exhibit a mixed style, combining aspects of the seventeenth and twentieth century formats.

Crime lab reports largely have a twentieth-century presentation and argument style. Some forensic scientists argue that the "facts speak for themselves" but, in reality, without an interpretation ("the Q1 paint sample could have come from the suspect vehicle,") there is no expert opinion—the very reason a forensic scientist goes to court. In court, however, the report and the testimony take on a very seventeenth-century style. The expert testifies to what they did and how they did it; a large part of their credibility comes from their professional experience.

Forensic science reports from different laboratories often have conflicting styles with no standard format. They are even dissimilar even to "standard" scientific article format: No abstract, no introduction, no materials and methods, and no references. Reports should contain the following:

- Name and address of the laboratory
- Case identifier (number)
- Name, address, and identifier of the contributor
- Date of receipt of evidence
- Date of report
- Descriptive list of submitted evidence
- Identification of the methodology
- Identity and signature of examiner
- Results and conclusions

The case file should contain documentation that supports the results and conclusions in the report. That documentation should include data obtained through the analytical process as well as information regarding the packaging of the evidence upon receipt and the condition of the evidence. All documentation generated during an examination must be preserved according to the written policy of the forensic laboratory, including paper, electronic files, standards, controls, observations, the results of the tests, charts, graphics, photographs, printouts, and communications.

Forensic laboratories review a percentage—and in some cases 100%—of cases prior to the report being issued. A case review should be conducted by a minimum of two personnel and the review should consist of a technical review and an administrative review. A technical review should be conducted on the report and the notes and data supporting the report must be reviewed independently by a technically competent peer.

Once a report has been reviewed, initials or other appropriate markings must be maintained in the case file by the personnel conducting the review. An administrative review should be conducted on the report to ensure adherence to laboratory policy and editorial correctness. Laboratory administration will determine the course of action if an examiner and the reviewer fail to agree.

While science is a public endeavor, police investigations are often a matter of discretion. Scientists are accustomed to scrutiny by other scientists and the public. Forensic scientists also face scrutiny in courtroom by the attorneys, the jury, and the judge.

Testimony

Not every case that a forensic scientist works will go to trial. In fact, opportunities for testifying may be infrequent and irregular. A case may not go to trial for a number of reasons: The defendant may plead guilty; plea arrangement may be made for a lesser sentence; the attorney may decide the evidence is not needed for trial; or the charges may be dropped.

The first notice that a forensic scientist will be required for testimony will often be a *subpoena*, an official request from the court that he or she appears before it. The word is Latin for "under punishment," and if a subpoena is ignored, the scientist may face jail or additional penalties. The subpoena tells the defendant's name, the jurisdiction, the date and time the scientist is requested to appear, and contact information for the requesting attorney.

When forensic scientists step into a courtroom to testify, they are, in essence, entering a foreign realm where only some of the rules of science apply. The legal arena has its own rules and most, but not all, apply to experts and they must abide by the rules. Experts have leeway in the courtroom that no other witnesses have. It is a strange intersection between science and the law where even the same words have different meanings. Take for example the word "error." To a scientist, error is something that occurs naturally in all measurements and is accounted for in the statistics that are generated, such as "standard error of the mean." Errors, in science, cannot be avoided and are reported in due process. An attorney, on the other hand, hears the word "error" and thinks: *Mistake!* The scientist has just admitted to doing something wrong, in the lawyer's view, and has opened the door for further questioning. This "clash of cultures" does not always serve either side very well and may obscure what both parties seek.

Ordinary witnesses may only testify to what they have directly experienced through their five senses. This testimony must be factual in nature and the witness, in nearly all cases, is barred from offering opinions, conjectures, or hypothetical information. Unlike other types of witnesses, however, expert witnesses are allowed to offer their opinions about evidence or situations that fall within their area of expertise. These opinions are allowed because the scientist is an expert in that area and knows more than anyone else in the courtroom about that topic; their opinion and expertise will assist the trier of fact in deciding the case.

Scientific evidence can be powerful; it can also be suspect. Judges and juries may not accept an expert's opinion as evidence because it is just that: The expert's view on that issue. Often, however, those opinions and views are based on solid scientific data generated through valid analyses and therefore have a firm basis in fact. Expert witnesses must always tread a fine line between their science and the potential for advocacy in a case.

When a forensic scientist testifies, he or she does so as an expert witness, that is, someone who knows more about a topic or subject than the average person. The scientist is brought to court by either the prosecution or defense and offered as an expert in some area of study that will aid the judge or jury (generically referred to as "the trier of fact") in reaching their verdict. The scientist then undergoes a process of establishing his or her education, training, experience, and expertise in that discipline; this process is called *voir dire*, which is Old French for "speak the truth" and is pronounced "vwa deer." Voir dire is a process where the attorneys, and occasionally the judge, question the scientist about their education, training, and experience. The scientist will often need to cite their educational degrees, work history, previous testimony experience, publications, professional associations, and other relevant information that will justify their expertise to the court. The attorney offering the scientist as an expert asks questions that will lay a foundation for the scientist's credentials; the opposing attorney then asks questions that may confirm or weaken that foundation. It is important for the scientist to provide *relevant* qualifications to the court: For example, being coach of the local high school soccer team has no bearing on whether someone should be considered an expert on drug analysis.

If the court rules that the scientist does possess sufficient credentials, he or she may testify on that subject in the case at hand. The scientist must be careful to remain within the bounds of their expertise. It may be tempting for the scientist to answer questions at the margin of their experience and offer speculative answers to be helpful or sound authoritative—*but they should not do it!* Few things will diminish a forensic scientist's expertise in the jury's minds faster than overexpertise. It is always better for an expert to answer truthfully, "I don't know" than to exceed his or her limits of knowledge, training, or experience.

Notes

Chapter 1: History

1. *Daubert v Merrill Dow Pharmaceuticals, Inc.* 1993, United States. p. 579.
2. National Institute of Justice, *Forensic Science: Status and Needs*, U.S. Department of Justice, Editor. 1999, U.S. Government Printing Office.
3. E.A. Poe, *Treasury of World Masterpieces*, 1981, Donnelly and Sons, New York. p. 69.
4. Ibid., p. 67.
5. C. Wilson, and D. Wilson, *Written in Blood*. 2003, New York: Carroll & Graf.

Chapter 2: The Nature of Evidence

1. S. Ryland and M.M. Houck, "Only Circumstantial Evidence," in *Mute Witnesses*, ed. M.M. Houck, 2001, San Diego, CA: Elsevier: Academic Press, 117–138.
2. R.D. Koons et al., "Forensic Glass Comparisons," in *Forensic Science Handbook*, ed. R. Saferstein, 2002, Upper Saddle River, NJ: Prentice-Hall, 161–213.
3. M.M Houck, "Intercomparison of Unrelated Fiber Evidence," *Forensic Science International*, 135 (2003): 146-149.
4. S. Ryland et al., "Discrimination of 1990s Original Automotive Paint Systems: A Collaborative Study of Black Nonmetallic Base Coat/Clear Coat Finishes Using Infrared Spectroscopy," *Journal of Forensic Sciences* 46 (1) (2001): 1–4.
5. R. Bisbing, "Forensic Hair Comparisons," in *Forensic Science Handbook*, ed. R. Saferstein, 2002, Englewood Cliffs, NJ: Prentice-Hall.
6. R.C. Murray, *Evidence from the Earth*, 2004, Missoula, MT: Mountain Press Publishing Company.
7. M. Hugos, *Essentials of Supply Chain Management*, 2003, New York: John Wiley and Sons.

Chapter 3: Pathology

1. *Oxford English Dictionary*, 2005, Oxford, UK: Oxford University Press.
2. K. Iverson, *Death to Dust: What Happens to Dead Bodies?* 2nd ed. 2001, Tucson, AZ: Galen Press Ltd.
3. C. Wilson and D. Wilson, *Written in Blood*, 2003, New York: Carroll & Graf.
4. J. Thorwald, *The Century of the Detective*, 1965, New York: Brace & World Inc.
5. K.A. Collins and P.E. Lantz, "Interpretation of Fatal, Multiple, and Exiting Gunshot Wounds by Trauma Specialists," *Forensic Science International*, 65 (1994): 185–193.

6. J. Thorwald, *The Century of the Detective,* 1964, New York: Harcourt, Brace & World.

7. D.E. Dolinak Matshes and E. Lew, *Forensic Pathology: Principles and Practice,* 2005. Amsterdam: Elsevier.

8. W. Schneck, "Cereal Murder in Spokane," in *Trace Evidence Analysis: More Cases from Mute Witnesses,* ed., M.M. Houck, 2003, Academic Press: San Diego, CA.

9. D.H. Ubelaker and H. Scammell, *Bones: A Forensic Detective's Casebook,* 1st ed., 1992, New York Edward Burlingame Books, xiii, 317.

10. K.G.V. Smith, *A Manual of Forensic Entomology,* 1987, Ithaca, NY: Cornell University Press, 205.

11. E.P. Catts and N.H. Haskell, *Entomology and Death: A Procedural Guide,* 1990, Clemson, SC: Joyce's Print Shop.

12. G. Hutchins et al., "Practice Guidelines for Autopsy Pathology, *Archives of Pathology and Laboratory Medicine,* 123 (1999): 1085–1092.

Chapter 4: Fingerprints

1. S.A. Cole, *Suspect Identities,* 2001, Cambridge: Harvard University Press.

2. C. Wilson and D. Wilson, *Written in Blood,* 2003, New York: Carroll & Graf.

3. D. Ashbaugh, *Quantitative-Qualitative Friction Ridge Analysis: An Introduction to Basic and Advanced Ridgeology,* 1999, Boca Raton, FL: CRC Press.

4. B. Carlson, *Human Embryology and Developmental Biology Updated Edition,* 2003, Amsterdam: Elsevier.

5. M.M. Houck, "Playing Fast and Loose with Time and Space: Statistics and Forensic Science," in *Joint Statistical Meetings,* 2006, Seattle, WA: American Statistical Association.

6. P. Komarinski, *Automated Fingerprint Identification Systems,* 2005, San Diego, CA: Elsevier: Academic Press.

Chapter 5: Trace Evidence

1. M.M. Houck, "Foreword—The Grammar of Forensic Science," *Forensic Science Review,* 18 (2) (2006).

2. M.M. Houck and J.A. Siegel, *Fundamentals of Forensic Science,* 2006, San Diego, CA: Elsevier: Academic Press.

3. M.M. Houck, *Mute Witnesses.* 2001, San Diego, CA: Elsevier: Academic Press.

4. M.M. Houck, *Trace Evidence Analysis.* 2001, San Diego, CA: Elsevier: Academic Press.

5. SWGMAT, "Trace Evidence Recovery Guidelines," *Forensic Science Communications,* 1 (3) (1999), available at www.fbi.gov.

6. R. Bisbing, "Forensic Hair Comparisons," in *Forensic Science Handbook,* ed. R. Saferstein, 2002, Englewood Cliffs, NJ: Prentice-Hall.

7. M.M. Houck and C. Koff, "Racial Assessment in Hair Examinations," in *International Association of Craniofacial Identification,* 2000, Washington, DC: Federal Bureau of Investigation.

8. B.D. Gaudette and E.D. Keeping, "An Attempt at Determining Probabilities in Human Scalp Hair Comparison," *Journal of Forensic Sciences,* 19 (1974): 599–606.

9. B.D. Gaudette, "Probabilities and Human Pubic Hair Comparisons," *Journal of Forensic Sciences,* 21 (1976): 514–517.

10. R.A. Wickenheiser and D.G. Hepworth, "Further Evaluation of Probabilities in Human Scalp Hair Comparisons," *Journal of Forensic Sciences,* 35 (1990): 1323–1329.

11. B.D. Gaudette, "Strong Negative Conclusions: A Rare Event," *Canadian Society of Forensic Science Journal,* 18 (1985): 32–37.

12. M.M Houck and B. Budowle, "Correlation of Microscopic and Mitochondrial DNA Analysis of Hairs," *Journal of Forensic Sciences,* 45 (5) (2002): 1–4.

13. J.R. Aspland, "What Are Dyes? What Is Dyeing?" in *AATCC Dyeing Primer.* 1981, Research Triangle Park, North Carolina: American Association of Textile Chemists and Colorists.

14. SWGMAT, "Scientific Working Group on Materials Analysis: Forensic Fiber Analysis," *Forensic Science Communications,* 1 (1) (1999).

15. E. Locard, *Manual of Police Techniques,* 3rd ed., 1939, Paris: Payot.

16. H.A. Deadman, "Fiber Evidence and the Wayne Williams Trial: Part I," *FBI Law Enforcement Bulletin,* 53 (3) (1984): 12–20.

17. H.A. Deadman, "Fiber Evidence and the Wayne Williams Trial: Part II," *FBI Law Enforcement Bulletin,* 53 (5) (1984): 10–19.

18. D.W. Deedrick, "Searching for the Source: Car Carpet Fibres in the O.J. Simpson case," *Contact,* 26 (1998): 14–16.

19. M.M. Houck, *Mute Witnesses,* 1999, San Diego, CA: Elsevier: Academic Press.

20. K. Hatch, *Textile Science,* 1993, St. Paul, MN: West Publishing.

21. B.D. Gaudette, "Forensic Fiber Analysis," in *Forensic Science Handbook, Volume 3,* ed. R. Saferstein, 1993, Englewood Cliffs, NJ: Prentice-Hall, Inc.

22. G.R. Carroll, "Forensic Fibre Microscopy," in *Forensic Examinations of Fibres,* ed. J. Robertson, 1992, New York: Ellis Horwood, 99–126.

23. P. Apsell, "What Are Dyes? What Is Dyeing?" in *AATCC Dyeing Primer,* 1981, Research Triangle Park, North Carolina: American Association of Textile Chemists and Colorists.

24. R.L. Connelly, "Colorant Formation for the Textile Industry," in *Color Technology in the Textile Industry,* 1997, Research Triangle Park, North Carolina: American Association of Textile Chemists and Colorists, 91–96.

25. K.G. Wiggins, J.A. Holness, and B.M. March, "The Importance of Thin layer Chromatography and UV Microspectrophotometry in the Analysis of Reactive Dyes Released from Wool and Cotton Fibers," *Journal of Forensic Sciences,* 50 (2) (2005): 364–368.

26. M.C. Grieve, T. Biermann, and K.G. Wiggins, "Fiber Comparisons Using Microspectrophotometry," *Science and Justice,* 39 (4) (1999): 273.

27. M.W. Tungol, E.G. Bartick, and A. Montaser, "The Development of a Spectral Data Base for the Identification of Fibers by Infrared Microscopy," *Applied Spectroscopy,* 44 (1990): 543–549.

28. C. Roux and P. Margot, "An Attempt to Assess the Relevance of Textile Fibres Recovered from Car Seats," *Science and Justice,* 37 (1997): 225–230.

29. M.M. Houck, "Intercomparison of Unrelated Fiber Evidence," *Forensic Science International*, 135 (2003): 146–149.

30. S. Ryland, R.J. Kopec, and P.N. Somerville, "The Evidential Value of Automobile Paint. Part II: Frequency of Occurrence of Topcoat Colors," *Journal of Forensic Sciences*, 26 (1) (1981): 1–11.

31. G.P.A. Turner, *Introduction to Paint Chemistry and Principles of Paint Technology*, 1995, London: Chapman-Hall.

32. J. Bentley, "Composition, Manufacture and Use of Paint," in *Forensic Examination of Paint and Glass*, ed. B. Caddy, 2001, London: Taylor and Francis, 123–141.

33. S. Ryland et al., "Discrimination of 1990s Original Automotive Paint Systems: A Collaborative Study of Black Nonmetallic Base Coat/Clear Coat Finishes Using Infrared Spectroscopy," *Journal of Forensic Sciences*, 46 (1) (2001): 1–14.

34. SWGMAT, "Forensic Paint and Comparison Analysis Guidelines," *Forensic Science Communications*, 1 (2) (1999), available at www.fbi.gov.

35. SWGMAT, "Standard Guide for Using Scanning Electron Microscopy/ X-ray Spectrometry in Forensic Paint Examinations," *Forensic Science Communications*, 4 (4) (2002), available at www.fbi.gov.

36. SWGMAT, "Glass Fractures," *Forensic Science Communications*, 7 (1) (2005), available at www.fbi.gov.

37. J. Thornton, "Interpretations of Physical Aspects of Glass Evidence," in *Forensic Examination of Glass and Paint*, ed. B. Caddy, 2001, London: Taylor and Francis, 97–122.

38. R.D. Koons et al., "Forensic Glass Comparisons," in *Forensic Science Handbook*, ed. R. Saferstein, 2002, Upper Saddle River, NJ: Prentice-Hall, 161–213.

39. W.C. McCrone, L.B. McCrone, and J.G. Delly, eds., *Polarized Light Microscopy*. 1978, Ann Arbor, MI: Ann Arbor Science.

40. SWGMAT, "Glass Refractive Index Determination," *Forensic Science Communications*, 7 (1) (2005), available at www.fbi.gov.

41. SWGMAT, "Elemental Analysis of Glass," *Forensic Science Communications*, 7 (1) (2005), available at www.fbi.gov.

42. C. Wilson and D. Wilson, *Written in Blood*, 2003, New York: Carroll & Graf.

43. R.C. Murray, *Evidence from the Earth*, 2004, Missoula, MT: Mountain Press Publishing Company.

44. R.C. Murray and J.C.F. Tedrow, *Forensic Geology*, 1992, Englewood Cliffs, NJ: Prentice-Hall. xiii, 203.

45. R.C. Murray and L.P. Solebello, "Forensic Examination of Soil," in *Forensic Science Handbook*, ed. R. Saferstein, 2002, Upper Saddle River, NJ: Prentice-Hall.

Chapter 6: DNA

1. R. McKie, "Meet the DNA Genius Who Fears the Dark Side of His Discovery," *Observer*, August 8, 2004: London.

2. N.I.o Justice, "Convicted by Juries, Exonerated by Science: Case Studies in the Use of DNA Evidence to Establish Innocence After Trial, ed., Department of Justice, 1996, Washington, DC: National Institute of Justice.

3. A.C. Mulkern, B. MacWilliams and T. Saavedra, "Falsely Jailed: What Happened?" in *Orange County Register*, 1996, 1.

4. S. Pfeifer, "Prosecutors Crack the Case Using Old-Fashioned Detective Work," in *Orange County Register*, 1996, 1.

5. J.M. Butler, *Forensic DNA Typing: Biology and Technology Behind STR Markers*, 2005, San Diego, CA: Elsevier: Academic Press.

6. National Institute of Justice, *Lessons Learned from 9/11: DNA Identification in Mass Fatality Incidents*, ed., U.S. Department of Justice, 2006, U.S. Department of Justice.

7. National Institute of Justice, *Using DNA to Solve Cold Cases*, ed., U.S. Department of Justice, 2002, U.S. Department of Justice.

8. M.M. Houck and B. Budowle, "Correlation of Microscopic and Mitochondrial DNA Analysis of Hairs," *Journal of Forensic Sciences*, 45 (5) (2002): 1–4.

9. S. Ryland and M.M. Houck, "Only Circumstantial Evidence," in *Mute Witnesses*, ed. M.M. Houck, 2001, San Diego, CA: Elsevier: Academic Press, 117–138.

10. National Institute of Justice, *Using DNA to Solve Cold Cases*, ed., U.S. Department of Justice, 2002, U.S. Department of Justice.

11. J.L. Peterson and M.J. Hickman, *Census of Publicly Funded Forensic Crime Laboratories, 2002*, Bureau of Justice Statistics, 2005, Department of Justice.

Chapter 8: Anthropology

1. D.H. Ubelaker and H. Scammell, *Bones: A Forensic Detective's Casebook*, 1st ed., 1992, New York: Edward Burlingame Books, xiii, 317.

2. D. Ubelaker, *Human skeletal remains*, 2000, Washington, DC: Taraxacum.

3. N. Sauer, "Manner of Death," in *Human Identification: Case Studies in Forensic Anthropology*, ed. T. Rathbun and J. Buikstra, 2000, Springfield, IL: Charles C. Thomas Publishers, 176–184.

Index

About the Author

MAX M. HOUCK is the Director of the Forensic Science Initiative, a program that develops research and professional training for forensic scientists and professionals in related fields. He is a trace evidence expert and forensic anthropologist who was assigned to the Trace Evidence Unit at the FBI Laboratory from 1992 to 2001. Houck is also Director of Forensic Business Development at West Virginia University and serves as Chairman of the Forensic Science Educational Program Accreditation Commission. He serves on the editorial boards of the *Journal of Forensic Sciences* and the *Journal of Forensic Identification*. He is the author or editor of *Fundamentals of Forensic Science, Mute Witnesses: Trace Evidence Analysis*, and other books and articles.